A Collection of Simple

ANGLO-INDIAN

Recipes

D1610468

A Collection of Simple
ANGLO-INDIAN
Recipes

*350 Recipes of Lip smacking, well loved,
traditional and popular Anglo-Indian Dishes.
Old forgotten dishes now revived to
suit present day tastes and palates*

by Bridget White

PARTRIDGE
A Penguin Random House Company

Print information available on the last page.

To order additional copies of this book, contact
Partridge India
000 800 10062 62
orders.india@partridgepublishing.com

www.partridgepublishing.com/india

Contents

VIII. ANGLO-INDIAN DESSERTS, CUSTARDS AND PUDDINGS

IX. THE ANGLO-INDIAN SNACK BOX

A. NIBBLES, FINGER FOOD, SMALL BITES, SAVOURIES & TEA TIME TREATS

FOREWORD

It gives me great pleasure to bring out this new publication entitled **'A COLLECTION OF SIMPLE ANGLO-INDIAN RECIPES'** which is a revised, consolidated version of 4 of my earlier Recipe Books, namely **Bridget's Anglo-Indian Delicacies, A Collection of Anglo-Indian Roasts, Casseroles and Bakes, The Anglo-Indian Snack Box and The Anglo-Indian Festive Hamper.**

More than 350 Recipes of traditional, popular and well loved, Anglo-Indian Dishes have been specially selected from these earlier Cookery Books and featured in this Omni-bus Edition. The huge selection of Anglo-Indian dishes featured in this Recipe Book will surely take one on a sentimental and nostalgic journey down memory lane of old forgotten Anglo-Indian Culinary Delights. *All the old dishes cooked during the time of the Raj have now been revived to suit present day tastes and palates.* This Recipe Book would also serve as a 'Ready Reckoner' and a useful guide for teaming up dishes for everyday Anglo-Indian Meals as well as for festive and special occasions.

So what are you waiting for? Delve into this awesome collection and you'll find simple and easy recipes for preparing your favorite Ox tail and Trotters Soups, Plain Pepper Water or Bone Pepper Water, Vindaloos and Curries, Devil Fries & Chops, Nana's Special Duck, Chicken, Beef & Pork Roasts, Beef and Chicken Country Captain, Papa Pat's Pork Chops, Mince Cutlets, Stews, Croquettes & Rissoles, Yellow Coconut Rice & Ball Curry, Junglee Palau & Vegetable Jalfrazie, Devil Chutney, Brinjal Pickle, Fish Padda and many more **ANGLO-INDIAN DELICACIES.**

Add that *'Anglo'* touch to your meal by baking a simple and tasty Shepherd's Pie, a Pot Luck Casserole, a Pork Mince Pie or any of the old 'one dish meals' that your grandma baked in your childhood. Choose the recipe for your favourite baked dish from **A COLLECTION OF ANGLO-INDIAN ROASTS, CASSEROLES AND BAKES.** The very names of the dishes will make you drool. Round it off with a creamy

Caramel Custard, Bread Pudding, Strawberry Flummery, Apple Grunt or any other lip-smacking Anglo-Indian Dessert or Sweet from the vast selection that has been featured.

Have a Party and serve your guests delicious Snacks, Short Eats and Nibbles from **THE *ANGLO-INDIAN SNACK BOX,*** that were the rage at 'Parties, Soirees and Elegant Evening Gatherings' in the olden days - all innovated and made famous by the Mogh Cooks of yore in the Tea Gardens in the Hills. Snack on Liver on Toast Squares, Scotch Eggs and Deviled Eggs, Cheese Straws, Mince Curry Puffs, Coconut Puffs, Mince Panthras, Fish Fingers, Fritters and a whole lot more,

What's your favourite childhood Christmas memory? Do you associate Christmas with the smells, sounds and sights of the season? This Cookery Book aims at just that. The separate section on **THE ANGLO-INDIAN FESTIVE HAMPER** features recipes of all the old Anglo-Indian Christmas favourites such as the Traditional Christmas Cakes, Plum Cakes, Mince Pies, Fruit Cakes, Kalkals, Rose Cookies, Coconut Sweets, the Christmas Pudding, Bole Cake, Semolina Cake, Dodol, Beveca, Marzipan Sweets, Peanut Fudge, Cashew nut Fudge, etc, etc. It will awaken long forgotten magical memories of childhood - Of the smell of the decorated Pine Christmas Tree in the Sitting Room, the enticing aroma of Christmas Cakes being baked, the Kalkals and Rose Cookies being fried and the aroma of the other Christmas Goodies being prepared in the kitchen by Mama and Nana - Memories of the whole family sitting round the dining table on "Kalkal Making Day" rolling the kalkals on the back of a fork or fighting to lick the left over cake batter in the mixing bowl will come flooding back. Recreate the Christmas of your childhood with these recipes of all the old Christmas Treats. Then to round off the festive spread, you could make your own home-made Grape and Ginger Wine.

The recipes in this book are simple and easy to follow and only easily available ingredients have been suggested. The easy-to-follow directions for preparing these old, popular, sumptuous dishes make cooking simple, enjoyable and problem-free.

All the recipes in this Book are for 6 generous servings. If cooking for a smaller or larger number, the quantities should be adjusted accordingly.

I

INTRODUCTION

A FEW TIPS ON HOW TO GET THE AUTHENTIC TASTE OF ANGLO-INDIAN DISHES COOKED BY GRANDMA

"The Joy of cooking begins with using the right ingredients"

In order to get the authentic and well remembered taste of Grandma's Anglo-Indian Curries and Side dishes, it is always advisable to use only the right ingredients that are called for in the recipe.

The secret of good, tasty cooking is the right proportion of ingredients that are to be used in cooking a particular dish. While preparing any dish, a perfectly balanced mix of the various ingredients should be maintained since adding even a little more or less can ruin it. Another important aspect is to extract the correct strength of a spice and never overstate it.

It is always advisable, to use good quality condiments and spices. Anglo-Indian Cooking specifically makes use of these commonly available ingredients: namely chillies, cumin, pepper, turmeric, coriander (either whole or in powder form) and whole spices. So ensure that the expiry date has not lapsed while shopping for these ingredients.

As far as possible use ginger and garlic paste that is ground at home in a blender using fresh root ginger and garlic. The readymade ginger and garlic paste available in stores around the world contain vinegar / acetic acid and other preservatives. These detract from the original taste of the Curry giving it a completely different flavour.

If fresh homemade ginger and garlic paste is not available, then Garlic Powder could be used instead of fresh garlic. One teaspoon of garlic powder is equal to a whole garlic, so half a teaspoon would suffice. Ginger powder too can be substituted for fresh ginger. One teaspoon of dry ginger powder mixed with ¼ cup of water is equal to 2 teaspoons of fresh ginger paste, so half a teaspoon of ginger powder would be equal to 1 teaspoon of fresh ginger paste.

Any good cooking oil could be used in the preparation of Anglo-Indian dishes such as Sun flower Oil, groundnut Oil or even Olive Oil depending on one's preference.

Use only White Non-Fruit Vinegar or Malt Vinegar in the dishes calling for Vinegar as fruit based vinegars could change the taste of the dish.

Avoid random garnishing of every dish with chopped coriander / cilantro / celery as these ingredients change the flavour and taste of a dish. Garnish only if the recipe says to do so.

Timing is also very important. A dish should never be under or over cooked or else it loses its flavours and nutrients.

Finally, follow the recipe for each dish scrupulously. Don't experiment by adding or changing ingredients as the dish wouldn't taste the way it should have. Each dish calls for certain ingredients and the spices and condiments should be used judiciously in each dish, so as to bring out the flavour and strength of each spice or ingredient. ***Therein lies the secret of ANGLO-INDIAN CUISINE***

To conclude in the words of Wolfgang Puck "Cooking is like Painting a Picture or Writing a Song. Just like there are only so many Colours or Notes, there are only so many flavours - It's how you combine them that sets you apart"

II

SOUPS AND BROTH

Soups have always been a basic Dinner Menu item. It became part of the Anglo-Indian Culinary repertoire during the days of the British Colonial Era. Delicious homemade soup is welcome any time whether ladled from a Tureen or a huge Crock Pot, as a heart-warming first course on a cold winter's evening, or served chilled as a refreshing start to a pleasant summer meal.

Featured in this section are recipes for a few old favorites that were extremely popular in the olden days.

1. THE ARMY CAMP CHICKEN SOUP

A hearty, lightly flavoured soup of chicken and vegetables that took its origins from the famous "Camp Soup" that was served during the War. This soup is excellent when you have a bad cold or 'feel down in the dumps'. Any vegetables of one's choice could be used in its preparation.

Serves 6   Time required: 1 hour

Ingredients
½ kg chicken cut into medium size pieces
2 carrots peeled and chopped into chunks
1 cup cauliflower florets
6 to 8 string beans broken into bits
2 onions chopped thickly
2 tomatoes chopped
1 teaspoon pepper corns
Salt to taste
1 bay leaf
1 teaspoon chopped garlic
1 teaspoon chopped mint

Place all the above ingredients in a suitable vessel or cock pot with 6 to 8 cups of water and bring to boil. Reduce heat and simmer for about 1 hour till the chicken is soft and tender and the soup thickens. (Alternately, pressure cook for about 10 minutes). Serve with steamed rice or bread.

2. COCK-A-LEEKIE SOUP (CHICKEN AND LEEK SOUP)

Cock-a-leekie soup was originally a Scottish Soup dish prepared mainly with Chicken, Barley and Onion Leeks hence the name 'Cock-a-Leekie. The original recipe called for the addition of prunes but it could be omitted. Beef or mutton can be substituted for Chicken if desired.

Serves 6   Time required: 1 Hour

Ingredients
1 kg chicken cut into medium size pieces without the skin
2 medium size onions chopped
½ cup Pearl Barley or Sago (soak in a little water for 30 minutes)

6 or 8 Onion Leeks
2 tablespoons chopped mint
1 teaspoon ground black pepper / pepper powder
Salt to taste
10 to 12 cups of water

Place all the ingredients in a suitable pan or crock pot. Cook first on high heat then reduce the heat to low and simmer till the chicken, barley and onion leeks are tender and the soup is thick. (Alternately, pressure cook for about 10 minutes). Serve with Bread or Dinner rolls.

3. THE BROWN SAHIB BEEF AND VEGETABLE SOUP

A delightful Beef and Vegetable Broth lightly flavoured with pepper, garlic and cumin. This was one of the early soups that originated during the time of the Raj.

Serves 6   Time required: 1 hour

Ingredients
½ kg beef with bones cut into medium size pieces
1 small cabbage coarsely cut
3 medium size carrots cut into medium size pieces
2 potatoes peeled and cut into quarters
3 tomatoes chopped
2 onions chopped thickly
2 teaspoons ground black pepper / pepper powder
1 teaspoon cumin powder
Salt to taste
1 teaspoon chopped garlic
2 teaspoons chopped mint

Boil all the above ingredients with about 2 litres of water on high heat for some time. Lower heat and simmer for 2 or 3 hours till the meat is well cooked and the broth is thick and a good brown colour. (Alternately, pressure cook for about 10 to 15 minutes). Serve with Bread or Buns.

4. MUTTON / LAMB BREAST BONE SOUP

This is a hearty and nutritious soup prepared from the Breast or Chest portion of the goat or sheep. This soup was always recommended by the older generation for those suffering from chest colds, bronchitis, back pain etc as well as expectant and nursing mothers and for those recovering after a serious illness or surgery

Serves 6   Time required: 1 hour

Ingredients
½ kg tender mutton or lamb bones from the breast portion with some meat on them
2 teaspoons ground black pepper / pepper powder
2 teaspoons chopped mint
2 large tomatoes chopped
2 onions sliced thickly
1 stick cinamon (about one inch)
Salt to taste

Rinse the bones and boil / pressure cook with all the other ingredients in sufficient water till the soup is thick. Add more salt and pepper if needed. Serve with bread.

5. CHICKEN MULLIGATAWNY SOUP

Mulligatawny Soup which originated during the days of the Raj as a 'Curried Soup" was actually the anglicized version of the Tamil "Melligu -Thani". (Melligu meaning pepper and Thani meaning water). As the name suggests it was originally a watery soup with the addition of Pepper. However in course of time a lot of other ingredients such as coconut, meat and other spices were added to give it a completely different flavour. This soup is a tasty meal in itself.

Serves 6   Time required: 1 hour

Ingredients
½ kg chicken chopped into medium size pieces
1 teaspoon chillie powder
2 teaspoons ground black pepper / / pepper powder

1 teaspoon cumin powder
1 teaspoon coriander powder
1 teaspoon crushed garlic
2 big onions sliced
3 tablespoons red lentils / masoor dhal
1 cup coconut paste or coconut milk
Salt to taste

Cook the chicken and all the ingredients with 6 to 8 cups of water in a large vessel on high heat till it reaches boiling point. Lower the heat and simmer for at least one hour till the soup is nice and thick. Alternately, pressure cook for about 15 minutes on medium heat. Add 2 teaspoons of butter while still hot. Garnish with mint leaves. Serve with bread or rice.

Note: Chicken could be substituted with Mutton or Lamb if desired.

6. LAMB (OR PORK) TROTTERS SOUP

Serves 6   Time required: 45 minutes

Ingredients
6 to 8 trotters (mutton or pork) each to be chopped into 2 pieces
2 or 3 green chilies (optional)
Salt to taste
1 teaspoon ground black pepper / pepper powder
1 teaspoon chillie powder
2 or 3 cloves
1 stick of cinamon (about one inch)
2 medium size tomatoes chopped into quarters
1 large onion chopped roughly

Wash the trotters well. Place all the above ingredients together with the trotters and sufficient water in a pressure cooker. Pressure cook for about 20 minutes or till the trotters are tender. Mix in a tablespoon of flour and simmer till the soup is fairly thick. Serve hot with bread. This is a very nourishing soup.

7. HEARTY OXTAIL AND ONION SOUP

This is another typical Anglo-Indian favourite. Bits of ox tail are simmered with onions and carrots to a nice thick broth which is both healthy and flavourful

Serves 6   Time required: 1 hour 30 minutes

Ingredients
1 oxtail chopped into medium size pieces
4 carrots peeled and chopped
3 onions chopped
2 teaspoons ground black pepper / pepper powder
Salt to taste
2 teaspoons butter
2 teaspoons chopped mint leaves
2 tomatoes chopped

Heat the butter in a pressure cooker. Fry the onions and carrots till light brown. Add the tomatoes and sauté for a few minutes till pulpy. Now add all the other ingredients and sufficient water. Pressure cook on medium heat for about 15 to 20 minutes, till the soup is thick and the oxtail is tender and soft. Garnish with chopped mint leaves. Serve with fried bread.

8. RED LENTIL VEGETABLE SOUP (DAL SOUP)

This is an easy to prepare healthy lentils and vegetable soup which is high in protein. It could be a tasty meal in itself.

Serves 6   Time required: 1 hour

Ingredients
3 tablespoons red lentils / masur dhal
2 carrots peeled and diced
5 or 6 runner beans cut into medium size pieces
1 cup cauliflower florets
½ cup green peas
2 medium size potatoes peeled and cut into small bits
1 bay leaf

1 piece (1 inch) cinnamon
2 cloves
½ teaspoon red chillie powder
½ teaspoon coriander powder
1 soup cube of any flavor
Salt to taste
1 teaspoon black pepper corns

Place all the above ingredients in a suitable crock pot or large pan together with 8 or 10 cups of water and bring to boil. Once it reaches boiling point, lower the heat and simmer till the vegetables are cooked. (Alternately, pressure cook for about 10 minutes). Garnish with chopped mint or parsley and a blob of butter or cream

III

ANGLO-INDIAN PEPPER WATER

Pepper Water is an important dish on the Anglo-Indian lunch table and is invariably prepared many times a week. It is always combined with Steamed White Rice and a dry non-vegetarian dish which could either be chicken, meat or sea food and most often a vegetable foogath as well. Pepper Water should always be of a watery consistency.

Pepper water can be stored in the refrigerator for a few days without spoiling due to the tamarind used in its preparation.

1. PLAIN PEPPER WATER

A simple and easy recipe to prepare the classic Anglo-Indian Pepper Water. Pepper Water is an important dish on the Anglo-Indian lunch table and is invariably prepared many times a week. Pepper water can be stored in the refrigerator for a few days without spoiling due to the tamarind used in its preparation.

Serves 6   Time required: 30 minutes

Ingredients
2 large tomatoes chopped
1 teaspoon ground black pepper / pepper powder
1 teaspoon chillie powder
1 teaspoon cumin powder
½ teaspoon turmeric powder
½ teaspoon coriander powder
Salt to taste
½ cup tamarind juice extracted from a small ball of tamarind
or 1 teaspoon tamarind paste

Cook all the above ingredients with 3 or 4 cups of water in a suitable vessel on high heat till it boils. Reduce the heat and cook on low heat for about 10 minutes. Temper the Pepper Water, as follows

To temper the Pepper Water: Heat 2 teaspoons oil in another vessel, add a teaspoon of mustard seeds. When they begin to splutter add a sliced onion, a few curry leaves, two broken red chilies and a teaspoon of chopped crushed garlic and sauté for a few minutes, till the onions turn light brown. Pour the pepper water into the seasoning and mix well. Turn off the heat. Serve hot with rice and any meat side dish.

Note: The pepper water can be prepared by using fresh red chilies cumin seeds coriander seeds, peppercorns ground in a mixer instead of the powders.

2. DOL PEPPER WATER (DHAL / LENTILS PEPPER WATER)

Serves 6   Time required: 45 minutes

Ingredients
1 Cup Tur or Masoor Dhal
2 cups of water
1 onion chopped
2 teaspoons chillie powder
1large tomato chopped
1 teaspoon cumin powder
1 teaspoon ground black pepper / pepper powder
1 teaspoon ginger garlic paste
½ teaspoon turmeric powder
1 teaspoon coriander powder
½ cup tamarind juice extracted from a small ball of tamarind or 1 teaspoon tamarind paste
Salt to taste

Cook the dhal with 2 cups of water till soft in a pressure cooker. Add all the above mentioned ingredients and sufficient water to the cooked dhal to make it a thin consistency and bring to boil. Cook on low heat for a few more minutes.

To temper the Dol / Dhal Pepper Water: Heat 2 teaspoons oil in another vessel, add a teaspoon of mustard seeds. When they begin to splutter add a sliced onion, a few curry leaves, two broken red chilies and sauté for a few minutes. Pour the dhal pepper water into the seasoning and mix well. Serve hot with steamed rice and pepper fry.

3. BONE PEPPER WATER

Serves 6   Time required: 45 minutes

Ingredients
½ kg soft bones and pieces of meat preferably from the breast portion either mutton or beef
2 teaspoons cumin powder

2 teaspoons chillie powder
1 teaspoon ground black pepper / pepper powder
1 teaspoon coriander powder
½ teaspoon turmeric powder
2 large onions chopped
2 large tomatoes chopped
Salt to taste
1 teaspoon crushed garlic
½ cup tamarind juice
½ cup coconut paste or coconut milk

Cook all the above ingredients with about 6 to 8 cups of water in a pressure cooker first on high heat then on low heat for ½ an hour or till the meat and bones are soft and the pepper water is quite thick.
Temper with mustard seeds, curry leaves and chopped onion. Garnish with coriander leaves. Serve hot with plain rice and any chutney.

4. HORSE GRAM PEPPER WATER

This Pepper water is prepared mostly by the Anglo-Indians in South India. Purported to be a very highly nutritious lentil dish, Horse Gram Pepper Water is good for those suffering from severe colds and chest complaints as it aids in clearing the throat and sinus.

Serves 6   Time required: 1 hour

Ingredients
1 cup of horse gram
2 teaspoons chillie powder
1 teaspoon cumin powder
1 teaspoons ground black pepper / pepper powder
1 teaspoon garlic paste
1 teaspoon coriander powder
1 cup light tamarind juice extracted from a small ball of tamarind
½ teaspoon turmeric powder

Soak the horse gram in water for a few hours. Wash well then pressure cook it with 3 cups of water and ½ teaspoon turmeric powder till soft.

Add the chillie powder, cumin powder, coriander powder, pepper powder, garlic paste, tamarind juice and salt and some more water and cook for 10 minutes on low heat. Remove from heat.

Temper with mustard seeds, curry leaves and chopped onion. Garnish with coriander leaves. Serve hot with plain rice and any chutney.

5. DRY SHRIMP PEPPER WATER

Serves 6   Time required: 40 minutes

Ingredients
1 teaspoon chillie powder
1 teaspoon cumin powder
1 teaspoon ground black pepper / pepper powder
½ teaspoon turmeric powder
2 tomatoes chopped
½ cup tamarind juice
Salt to taste
2 teaspoons dried shrimp powder

Puree the tomatoes and add 3 or 4 cups of water. Now add all the other ingredients except the shrimp powder. Boil for 10 minutes.
Temper the pepper water with mustard seeds, curry leaves, 2 red chilies broken into bits and half an onion. Add the shrimp powder and mix well. Serve Hot with rice.

IV

CURRIES, FRIES, SIDE DISHES ETC

A good curry depends on the right ingredients and the time taken to fry the onions and other ingredients which give it depth and body. The onions should be chopped or diced finely. This will ensure that the onions will fry evenly and create a base for the curry by combining the flavours of all the other ingredients. Take care however, not to burn the onions and garlic while frying or the curry would taste unpleasant.

While using dry spice powders, always mix them together with a little water before adding them to fried onions. This spice mixture should be fried on low heat for at least 3 or 4 minutes, to eliminate their raw taste. The delightful aroma will let you know when the spices are fried enough. If the spice mix looks dry and starts to burn, add a little more water or chopped tomatoes if the recipe calls for it. When the oil starts to separate from the mixture you could add the meat and fry it in this spice mix for five to ten minutes. This helps seal the meat slightly and retain its moisture.

Care should be taken to cook fresh and tender meat whenever possible. If the meat is marinated or mixed with the curry stuff or curry powder for some time before cooking, it not only locks in the flavours and juices but also helps to tenderize the meat so that cooking time is reduced considerably.

The recipes in this section cover, meat, chicken, pork, fish, eggs and vegetarian dishes which are all old favorites and very easy to prepare. Beef and veal can be substituted for chicken and mutton wherever desired. The pungency of the dishes can be adjusted according to individual taste by reducing or increasing the amount of chillie powder, spices or ground pepper suggested in each recipe.

A. MEAT

1. TYPICAL ANGLO-INDIAN BEEF CURRY
There's absolutely no stress or strain in preparing this delicious Beef curry. Just mix in all the ingredients and leave it to simmer on its own.

Serves 6   Time required: 45 minutes

Ingredients
½ kg beef from the Round Portion cut into medium size pieces
3 teaspoons chopped garlic
1 teaspoon chillie powder
3 onions sliced
Salt to taste
2 green chillies chopped
½ teaspoon turmeric powder
½ teaspoon ground black pepper / pepper powder
2 tablespoons oil
2 tablespoons vinegar

Add all the ingredients mentioned above to the meat and marinate for about 1 hour in a suitable pan or pressure cooker. Place the pan on high heat and cook closed for about 5 to 6 minutes. Lower the heat and mix well. Add enough water and then simmer for about 40 to 45 minutes till the meat is cooked and the gravy is thick.
(If cooking in a pressure cooker, turn off heat after 5 or 6 whistles. Open the cooker when the pressure dies down and simmer till the gravy thickens).
This curry can be served with bread, white steamed rice, hoppers, chapattis etc.

2. MAMA'S MANGO CHUTNEY MEAT CURRY (BEEF GLACEY)
An old Colonial dish, Meat Glassy, was also known as Mango Chutney Beef, and Fruity Meat Curry. It was probably one of the first experiments of the Khansamas / cooks during Colonial days. The term 'Glassy or Glazie' was a misrepresentation of the word 'Glace' by the cooks in the olden days. The addition of Mango chutney or fruit such as chunks of

sweet mango or pineapple in the curry, reduced the spiciness of the dish. Major Grey's Mango chutney, Col. Skinner's Mango Chutney and the Bengal Mango Chutney were normally used in the preparation of this Anglo-Indian dish in the olden days.

Serves 6   Time required: 1 hour

Ingredients
½ kg boneless Beef or Mutton cut into steaks
3 large onions sliced finely
2 tablespoons Sweet Mango Chutney (any brand) or 1 cup of mango or pineapple chunks
2 large tomatoes chopped finely or 2 tablespoons tomato puree
2 teaspoons ginger garlic paste
2 tablespoons vinegar
1 tablespoon Worcestershire sauce
2 one inch pieces cinnamon
1 Bay leaf
1 teaspoon ground black pepper
2 teaspoons chillie powder
Salt to taste
1 tablespoon plain flour
3 tablespoons oil

Flatten the beef or mutton with a mallet to break the fibers. Marinate the meat with the flour, a pinch of salt and pepper, and ½ teaspoon of ginger garlic paste for about one hour.
Heat oil in a pan and fry the marinated meat (a few pieces at a time) till brown and half cooked. Remove and keep aside.
In the same pan, (add a little more oil if desired) fry the onions, Bay leaf and cinnamon till golden brown. Add the ginger garlic paste, pepper, chillie powder, vinegar, Worcestershire sauce and tomato and fry well on low heat for a few minutes till the oil separates from the mixture. Add the fried meat pieces and mix well so that all the pieces are covered with the mixture. Add 2 cups of water and cook on low heat till the meat is tender and the gravy thickens. Now add the Sweet mango Chutney or fruit and mix well. Cover the pan and simmer for 2 or 3 more minutes, then remove from heat. Serve with steamed white rice or as a side dish with bread.

3. BEEF COUNTRY CAPTAIN

This is an old Colonial Anglo-Indian Recipe which was a favourite with the young and the old. It can also be prepared with left over Beef Roast or Chicken

Serves 6   Time required 45 minutes

Ingredients

½ kg tender Beef Undercut chopped into small pieces
6 peppercorns
2 big onions sliced
2 pieces cinnamon about one inch each
3 cloves
4 red chilies broken into bits
1 teaspoon chillie powder
½ teaspoon turmeric powder
1 teaspoon cumin powder
1teaspoon ginger garlic paste
Salt to taste
2 tablespoons oil
2 tablespoons vinegar
1 tablespoon butter or ghee
2 potatoes boiled, peeled and cut into quarters

Mix the meat with all the above ingredients in a suitable pan except the potatoes. Place the pan on high heat and fry for a few minutes till the pieces of meat turn firm. Add sufficient water and cook on medium heat till the meat is tender and all the gravy dries up. Mix in the boiled potatoes and butter / ghee then remove from heat. Serve with Rice or bread

Note: If cooking in a pressure cooker switch off heat after 5 or 6 whistles

4. BEEF / MUTTON / LAMB VINDALOO

Serves 6   Time required 45 minutes

Ingredients
½ kg beef from the Round Portion or mutton cut into medium pieces

3 big tomatoes pureed
2 big onions chopped
3 medium potatoes peeled and cut into quarters
3 tablespoons oil
Salt to taste
1 teaspoon mustard seeds powdered
2 teaspoons chillie powder
2 teaspoons cumin powder
1 teaspoon ground black pepper / pepper powder
2 teaspoons ginger garlic paste
½ cup vinegar
½ teaspoon turmeric powder

Heat oil in a suitable pan or pressure cooker and fry the onions till golden brown. Add the ginger garlic paste and fry well. Mix the chillie powder, turmeric powder, cumin powder, mustard powder and pepper powder with a little water and add to the onions. Fry well till the oil separates from the mixture. Add the tomato puree and salt and fry for some more time. Now add the beef, potatoes and vinegar and mix well. Add more water depending on how much gravy is required and cook till done. Serve with bread or rice.

5. BEEF / MUTTON GREEN CHILLIE FRY

Serves 6   Time required: 1 hour

Ingredients
1 kg tender Beef Undercut or mutton cut into medium size pieces
3 large onions sliced
1 large capsicum / bell pepper cut into small pieces (optional)
3 or 4 green chillies chopped
1 teaspoon chillie powder
1 tablespoon chopped garlic
½ teaspoon turmeric powder
Salt to taste
3 tablespoons oil

Boil the meat with turmeric powder and a little salt in sufficient water till tender. Keep aside.

Heat oil in a pan and fry the onions, chopped garlic, green chillies and capsicum for about 2 or 3 minutes. Add the cooked meat and all the other ingredients and mix well. Simmer till all the soup dries up. Stir fry till the oil leaves the sides of the pan. Serve as a side dish with rice and pepper water or with bread or chappatis.

6. BEEF / MUTTON MINCE BALL CURRY (KOFTA CURRY)

This is a typical Anglo-Indian Favourite. It can be prepared with either ground beef, mutton or lamb. It took its origins from the early Dutch settlers who were the first to introduce Forced Meat in India which eventually evolved into the forced meat balls being cooked in a gravy sauce which is our very own Anglo-Indian Ball Curry today. Ball Curry is also known as Bad Word Curry as word 'Ball' was considered a slang word or bad word in the olden days. Hence the name Bad Word Curry

Serves 6   Time required: 1 hour

Ingredients; For the Curry
3 large onions chopped
1 sprig curry leaves
3 teaspoons chillie powder
1 ½ teaspoons coriander powder
3 teaspoons ginger garlic paste
3 big tomatoes pureed
½ cup ground coconut paste
1 teaspoon spice powder or garam masala
Salt to taste
3 tablespoons oil
1 teaspoon coriander leaves chopped finely for garnishing
½ teaspoon turmeric powder

Ingredients for the Meat Balls (Koftas)
½ kg fine beef mince or lamb / mutton mince
½ teaspoon spice powder
3 green chilies chopped

A small bunch of coriander leaves chopped finely
Salt to taste
½ teaspoon turmeric powder

Heat oil in a large pan and fry the onions till golden brown. Add the ginger garlic paste and the curry leaves and fry for some time. Now add the chillie powder, coriander powder, spice powder or garam masala powder, turmeric powder and coconut and fry for a few minutes till the oil separates from the mixture. Now add the tomato juice and salt and simmer for some time. Add sufficient water and bring to boil.

Meanwhile get the meat balls ready. Mix the spice powder, salt, chopped green chilies, turmeric powder and coriander leaves with the mince and form into small balls. When the curry is boiling slowly drop in the mince balls carefully one by one. Simmer on slow heat for 20 minutes till the balls are cooked and the gravy is not too thick. Serve hot with Coconut Rice and Devil Chutney.

7. BEEF MINCE FRY

This is a quick and easy dish to cook when one has a packet of mince handy in the fridge but not too keen on making a Ball Curry. This simple and tasty dish could be eaten with Rice or Chapattis. Any meat mince such as beef, mutton, lamb or even chicken mince could be used. Green Peas, chopped cabbage, carrot, cauliflower, fenugreek / methi / venthium greens etc could be added to give the dish a twist.

Serves 6   Time required: 45 minutes

Ingredients
½ kg Beef Mince / Ground Beef
2 big onions chopped
½ teaspoon turmeric powder
1 teaspoon chopped garlic
1 teaspoon chopped ginger
2 green chilies chopped finely
2 tablespoons chopped coriander leaves
2 tablespoons oil

Salt to taste
½ teaspoon chillie powder

Heat oil in a pan and fry the onions till golden brown. Add the chopped ginger, garlic, green chilies and sauté for 3 minutes. Add the minced meat, turmeric powder, chillie powder and salt and mix well. Add the chopped coriander leaves and cook on low heat for about 15 to 20 minutes, till the mince is cooked and all the water evaporates. Simmer on low heat till the mince is dry and gives out a nice aroma. Serve hot with bread or chapattis as a side dish with Rice and Pepper water

8. TYPICAL ANGLO-INDIAN BEEF FRY
This simple dish is prepared very frequently in most Anglo-Indian homes. It goes well steamed rice and Pepper Water or Bread

Serves 6   Time required: 1 hour

Ingredients
1 kg good beef undercut, cut into medium size pieces
4 green chillies
3 big onions sliced
1 teaspoon finely chopped ginger
2 teaspoons finely chopped garlic
2 teaspoons chillie powder
1` teaspoon coriander powder
Salt to taste
½ teaspoon turmeric powder
3 tablespoons oil

Boil the meat in a little water, salt and a pinch of turmeric till tender. Remove the boiled meat and keep the remaining soup aside. Heat oil in a pan and fry the ginger, garlic and onions till golden brown. Add the cooked meat, chillie powder, turmeric powder, coriander powder and salt and mix well. Add the remaining soup and cook on low heat till all the soup dries up and the meat is brown. Serve with steamed rice and Pepper Water or Bread

9. MEAT DEVIL FRY

Serves 6   Time required:1 hour

Ingredients
1 kg Beef (tenderloin) or mutton cut into small cubes
3 onions chopped finely
3 tablespoons chopped coriander leaves
2 teaspoons chillie powder
1 teaspoon ground black pepper / pepper powder
1 medium size tomato chopped
1 tablespoon ginger garlic paste
Salt to taste
4 tablespoons oil

Place all the above ingredients with 2 cups of water in a pressure cooker and pressure cook on medium heat for about 12 to 15 minutes (6 to 8 whistles). Turn off heat and let the pressure die down. Open the pressure cooker and simmer on low heat till all the gravy dries up. Garnish with chopped coriander leaves. Serve as a side dish with Rice and Pepper Water

10. BEEF PEPPER FRY
Another popular and frequently made dish in Anglo-Indian homes

Serves 6   Time required: 45 minutes

Ingredients
½ kg tender Beef from the Round cut into small pieces
3 teaspoons fresh ground black pepper
1 teaspoon chopped ginger
2 big onions sliced finely
3 tablespoons oil
3 large potatoes peeled and cut into quarters
Salt to taste

Heat the oil in a pan and sauté the onions and chopped ginger for a few minutes. Add the meat, salt and pepper powder and mix well. Fry for 5 minutes on low heat turning the meat well till the pieces get firm. Add the potatoes and sufficient water and cook till the meat is soft. Continue simmering on low heat till all the water is absorbed and the meat and potatoes are brown. Serve hot with bread or rice.

11. BEEF PEPPER STEAKS

Serves 6   Time required: 45 minutes

Ingredients
1kg Beef Undercut cut into steaks
1 teaspoon turmeric powder
3 or 4 teaspoons fresh ground black pepper powder
3 tablespoons oil
2 big onions sliced finely
2 big tomatoes chopped
Salt to taste

Wash the meat well and marinate it with the pepper powder, salt and turmeric powder in a flat plate. Pour the oil on top and keep it over night in the refrigerator (or for about 4 hours before cooking), Pressure cook for just 5 minutes or cook in a pan for about 15 minutes. Add the onions and tomatoes and continue frying on low heat till the tomatoes turn pulpy and the steaks are a nice brown colour. Serve hot with boiled vegetables and bread.

12. BEEF MASALA STEAK

Serves 6   Time required:1 hour

Ingredients
1 kg Beef Steaks from the Flank Portion
1 teaspoon ground black pepper / black pepper powder
2 teaspoons Chillie Powder
1 teaspoon ginger garlic paste
1 teaspoon cumin powder
1 teaspoon coriander powder
Salt to taste

3 tablespoons oil
2 teaspoons vinegar

Marinate the steaks with all the above ingredients and keep aside for 2 hours. Transfer to a suitable pan and cook on low heat till the steaks are tender. Remove from heat. Heat some butter or ghee on a flat pan and brown each steak separately for a few minutes. Serve with mashed potatoes and browned onions.

13. BRAISED BEEF STEAK

Serves 6   Time required: 1 hour

Ingredients
1 Kg Beef Steaks cut from the Round Portion
2 teaspoons ground black pepper / black pepper powder
2 teaspoons chillie powder
½ teaspoon turmeric powder
3 onions sliced finely
1 teaspoon Mustard Powder or paste
3 tablespoons oil
Salt to taste
1 tablespoon Worcestershire Sauce or Tomato ketchup

Flatten the Steaks by beating with a mallet or cleaver. Marinate the steaks with all the above ingredients and leave aside for 2 or 3 hours. Heat a pan and cook the steaks first on high heat then on low heat till tender. (Add some water if required). Serve with Bread and Mashed Potatoes.

14. BEEF PEPPER CHOPS

Serves 6   Time required: 45 minutes

Ingredients
½ kg good Beef Rib Chops (Flatten them)
3 or 4 potatoes boiled, peeled and each cut in half lengthwise

4 big onions sliced
2 green chilies slit lengthwise (optional)
2 teaspoons ground black pepper / pepper powder
Salt to taste
3 tablespoons oil

Pressure cook the chops with a little water till tender letting some soup remain. Open the pressure cooker and add the onions, green chilies, salt, pepper powder and oil and mix well. Keep cooking on low heat till the soup dries up and the onions and meat are a nice brown colour. Just before turning off the heat add the boiled potatoes and mix once so that the gravy / sauce covers the potatoes. Serve hot with bread or rice.

15. BEEF OR VEAL MASALA CHOPS

Serves 6   Time required: approx 1 hour

Ingredients
1 kg good beef chops with a little fat (Flatten them)
3 or 4 potatoes, (boiled, peeled and cut in half lengthwise)
4 big onions sliced
2 green chilies slit lengthwise
2 teaspoons chillie powder
2 teaspoons cumin powder
2 tablespoons vinegar
1 teaspoon garlic paste
Salt to taste
3 tablespoons oil

Marinate the chops with all the above ingredients (except the onions and potatoes) and keep aside for 2 hours. Heat the oil in a suitable pan and add the marinated chops and mix well. Cook the chops with sufficient water till tender letting some soup remain. Mix in the sliced onions. Keep cooking on low heat till the soup dries up and the meat is a nice brown colour. Just before turning off the heat add the boiled potatoes and mix once so that the mixture covers the potatoes. Serve hot with bread or rice.

16. BEEF GRILL

Serves 6   Time required: 1 hour

Ingredients
1 kg Beef Undercut cut into fairly big pieces
2 teaspoons ground black pepper / pepper powder
2 teaspoons chillie powder
½ teaspoon turmeric powder
1 teaspoon cumin powder
1 teaspoon coriander powder
2 teaspoons ginger garlic paste
3 tablespoons vinegar
4 onions sliced in rounds
3 potatoes peeled and cut into halves
Salt to taste
3 tablespoons oil

Marinate the meat in vinegar, salt, pepper powder, chillie powder, ginger and garlic paste, turmeric powder, cumin powder and coriander powder and leave aside for about one hour.
Heat some of the oil in a suitable pan or pressure cooker and add the marinated meat. Fry well till the meat becomes firm. Add the potatoes and just enough water for the meat to cook. Simmer till all the gravy dries up. Remove the meat and potatoes and keep aside. Add a little more oil in the same pressure cooker or vessel and fry the onions till brown. Add the cooked meat and potatoes and mix well. Simmer for about 5 more minutes then take down. Serve with Bread or chapattis.

17. THE GREAT INDIAN PENINSULAR RAILWAY MEAT CURRY

The Railway Meat Curry is a direct throw back to the days of the British Raj, when travelling by train was considered aristocratic. As its very name suggests, this very popular and tasty dish was prepared and served with Bread or Dinner Rolls in Railway Refreshment Rooms and Dining Cars on long distance trains This wonderful curry was first served on the long distance train between Bombay to Calcutta. and in the Refreshment Rooms on Victoria Terminus Station in erstwhile Bombay

Serves 6   Time required: 1 hour 15 minutes

Ingredients
½ kg tender meat (Beef, mutton or lamb) cut into medium size pieces
6 peppercorns
2 big onions sliced finely
2 medium size tomatoes chopped
2 pieces cinnamon (about one inch in size)
2 cloves
4 red chilies broken into bits
2 teaspoons chillie powder
1 teaspoon cumin powder
1teaspoon ginger garlic paste
Salt to taste
2 tablespoons oil
2 tablespoons vinegar or ½ cup of tamarind juice

Mix the meat with the ginger garlic paste, salt, chillie powder and cumin powder and keep aside. Heat oil in a suitable pan or pressure cooker and fry the onions, red chillies and whole spices till golden brown. Add the meat and chopped tomato and mix well. Fry for a few minutes till the tomatoes turn pulpy. Add sufficient water and cook first on medium heat then on low heat till the meat is tender. Now add the the vinegar / Tamarind juice and simmer till the gravy is thick and dark brown.
Serve with steamed white rice or bread

18. MEAT AND DUMPLING STEW

Serves 6   Time required: 1 hour

Ingredients
½ kg beef undercut or mutton cut into medium pieces
3 carrots, 4 French beans, 1 small cauliflower cut into florets, 2 potatoes
2 green chilies slit lengthwise
2 medium size tomatoes chopped
1 big onion sliced
2 teaspoons ginger garlic paste
2 cloves, 2 pieces of cinnamon

6 or 7 pepper corns
A few mint leaves
Salt to taste
2 tablespoons oil
2 tablespoons coconut paste (optional)
2 tablespoons plain flour

Wash and cut the vegetables into suitable pieces. Cook the meat and vegetables together with all the above ingredients **(except the oil, onions and flour)** with sufficient water till the meat is cooked.
Meanwhile make a thin paste of the flour with ¼ cup of water.
In another pan heat the oil and fry the onions till golden brown. Add the flour paste and fry along with the onions for some time. Add the cooked meat and vegetables and simmer for 5 minutes. Serve hot with bread or hoppers.

Note: For Dumpling Stew, make dumplings as follows and add along with the meat and vegetables while cooking.

To make the dumplings, you will need 1 cup of flour, 1 teaspoon butter and a pinch of salt.
Mix all together with a little water to form soft dough. Form into small balls and flatten slightly. Add to the stew while cooking.

19. BRAISED OX TONGUE

Serves 6   Time required: approx 1 hour

Ingredients
1 Ox Tongue
2 onions sliced
1 teaspoon coriander powder
1 teaspoon ground black pepper / pepper powder
1 teaspoon chillie powder
2 one inch pieces of cinnamon
3 tablespoons Oil
Salt to taste

Boil the ox tongue in salt water till tender in a pressure cooker. When slightly cold, remove the top white skin. Cut into slices.

Heat oil in a pan and sauté the onions and cinnamon till slightly brown. Add the chillie powder, coriander powder, pepper powder, a little salt and about 4 tablespoons of the tongue stock and fry for a few minutes. Now add the cooked slices of Ox Tongue and the remaining stock. Mix well and simmer on low heat for about 10 minutes. Serve with Bread or with rice.

20. HEARTY OXTAIL STEW

Serves 6   Time required: 1 hour

Ingredients
1 small oxtail cut into medium pieces
3 carrots, 4 French beans, 2 potatoes
2 green chilies slit lengthwise
2 medium size tomatoes chopped
1 big onion sliced
2 teaspoons ginger garlic paste
2 cloves
2 one inch pieces of cinnamon
6 or 7 pepper corns
A few mint leaves
Salt to taste
2 tablespoons oil
2 tablespoons coconut paste (optional)
2 tablespoons plain flour

Wash and cut the vegetables into suitable pieces.

Parboil the Oxtail pieces with a little salt in sufficient water in a suitable vessel or pressure cooker till soft. Now add the vegetables together with all the above ingredients **(except the oil, onions and flour)** with a little more water and simmer till the vegetables are cooked.

Meanwhile make a thin paste of the flour with ¼ cup of water.

In another pan heat the oil and fry the onions till golden brown. Add the flour paste and fry along with the onions for some time. Add the cooked oxtail and vegetables and simmer for 5 minutes. Serve hot with bread or hoppers.

21. LIVER PEPPER FRY

Serves 6   Time required: 40 minutes

Ingredients
½ kg beef or lamb liver sliced thinly
4 large onions chopped
2 teaspoons ground black pepper / black pepper powder
½ teaspoon turmeric powder
3 tablespoons oil
Salt to taste

Wash the liver and keep aside to drain. Heat the oil in a pan and sauté the onions lightly. Add the sliced liver, salt, turmeric powder and pepper powder and mix well. Cover and simmer on low heat till the liver is cooked. Add a little water while cooking if gravy is required. Serve hot with rice or toast.

22. BEEF MINCE POTATO CHOPS (MINCE & POTATO RISSOLES)
Spiced Beef Mince is encased in mashed potato and crumb fried. Beef could be substituted with mutton or lamb

Serves 6   Time required: 1 hour

Ingredients
½ kg fine beef mince (or mutton / lamb)
1 medium sized onion chopped finely
2 teaspoons ground black pepper / pepper powder
Salt to taste
3 tablespoons oil
1 egg beaten
2 tablespoons breadcrumbs
3 large potatoes

Boil the potatoes, remove the skin and mash well. Keep aside.
Cook the mince with the onions, pepper powder, salt and a little oil in a suitable pan till the mince is dry. Remove from heat and cool for some time.

Form the mashed potatoes into even sized balls. Make a depression in the center and fill with the pepper mince. Flatten each ball to form an oval cutlet. Dip each one in the beaten egg then roll in the breadcrumbs and shallow fry the cutlets on low heat till golden brown on both sides. Serve as a side dish or party snack

23. GRAVY CUTLETS (CUTLETS IN TOMATO GRAVY)
The cutlets are fried and then added to a tomato gravy. Gravy Cutlets were / are very popular in Calcutta and West Bengal and said to be a Parsi Dish originally, but adopted and adapted in Anglo-Indian Cuisine. (If desired, the cutlets and gravy could be served separately)

Serves 6   Time required: 1 hour

Ingredients for the Cutlets
½ kg Beef or Mutton Mince / Ground Beef or Lamb
I onion chopped finely
6 cloves garlic chopped
3 green chilies chopped finely
2 slices bread soaked in water and squeezed dry
3 tablespoons bread crumbs
2 eggs beaten separately
Salt to taste
3 tablespoons oil or ghee
2 teaspoons chillie powder
1 teaspoon cumin powder
1 teaspoon ground black pepper / pepper powder
1 tablespoon chopped coriander leaves

Cook the mince with the chopped onion, garlic and salt with a little water till completely dry. Mix in the soaked bread slices, salt, pepper, green chillies, chillie powder, cumin powder coriander leaves, 2 teaspoons breadcrumbs and 1 beaten egg. Mix well. Form into oval shaped cutlets. Heat the oil in a flat pan. Dip each cutlet in the remaining beaten egg and roll in breadcrumbs and shallow fry the Cutlets till brown on both sides. Keep aside

Ingredients for the Gravy
3 large onions chopped
3 teaspoons chillie powder
1 teaspoon coriander powder
2 teaspoons ginger garlic paste
3 big tomatoes pureed
1 teaspoon spice powder or garam masala
Salt to taste
3 tablespoons oil
3 teaspoons coriander leaves chopped finely for garnishing
½ teaspoon turmeric powder

Heat oil in a large pan and fry the onions till golden brown. Add the ginger garlic paste and fry for some time. Now add the chillie powder, coriander powder, spice powder or garam masala powder, salt, turmeric powder and tomato puree and fry for a few minutes till the oil separates from the mixture. Add sufficient water and bring to boil. Simmer on low heat till the gravy thickens then carefully add the cutlets one by one. Simmer on low heat for 2 or 3 more minutes then turn off the heat. Serve hot with either bread, rice or chapattis.

24. CALCUTTA KOBHIRAJI BEEF / MUTTON CUTLETS

Serves 6   Time required: 1 hour

Ingredients
½ kg Mutton Mince or Beef Mince
I onion chopped finely
6 cloves garlic chopped
3 green chilies chopped finely
2 slices bread soaked in water and squeezed dry
3 tablespoons bread crumbs
2 eggs beaten separately
Salt to taste
3 tablespoons oil or ghee
2 teaspoons chillie powder
1 teaspoon ground black pepper / pepper powder

1 teaspoon cumin powder
1 tablespoon chopped coriander leaves

Cook the mince with the chopped onion, garlic and salt with a little water till completely dry. Mix in the soaked bread slices, salt, pepper, green chillies, chillie powder, cumin powder coriander leaves, 2 teaspoons breadcrumbs and 1 beaten egg. Mix well. Form into oval shaped cutlets.

Heat the oil in a flat pan. Dip each cutlet in the remaining beaten egg, roll in breadcrumbs and shallow fry the Cutlets till brown on both sides. Serve hot with wedges of lemon and onion rings.

25. NANA'S BEEF ROAST WITH GRAVY

Serves 6   Time required: About 1 hour 20 minutes

Ingredients
2 kg Beef from the "Top Side or Rump Part" (one chunk)
3 large onions cut into quarters
3 teaspoons ground black pepper / pepper powder
Salt to taste
3 dried red chillies or 1 teaspoon Paprika flakes
2 pieces of cinnamon (about one inch size)
2 teaspoons Tomato sauce
2 teaspoons vinegar
3 tablespoons oil
3 large potatoes pealed
2 tablespoons butter or ghee

Marinate the chunk of beef with salt and pepper for about one hour. Heat the oil in a big Roasting Pan and add the chunk of meat. Fry on high heat for about 3 minutes, turning the meat on all sides till it changes colour. Add the onions, tomato sauce, vinegar, dry chillies, cinnamon, potatoes and sufficient water and simmer till the meat is tender. Strain away any excess soup and keep aside.

Add 2 tablespoons of butter or ghee and continue to simmer on low heat till the meat is nicely brown all over and the potatoes too are nicely roasted. Slice the meat and arrange on a serving platter.

Pour the remaining soup or stock back into the pan and mix in 2 tablespoons of flour. Cook till the gravy thickens, stirring all the time. Spoon this gravy on top of the slices of roast and serve the remaining gravy on the side along with the Roast Potatoes.
(Alternatively the meat could be cooked in a pressure cooker till soft and then browned in a pan).

26. BRAISED BEEF FLANK

Serves 6   Time required: About 1 hour 20 mins

Ingredients
2 Kg Beef Flank (one piece)
2 onions sliced
3 medium size Carrots peeled and cut into pieces
1 teaspoon coriander powder
1 teaspoon chillie powder
½ teaspoon spice powder or garam masala powder
3 tablespoons Oil
4 tablespoons red wine
Salt to taste

Boil the chunk of Beef Flank in salted water till tender. Drain away the excess soup / stock and cut the boiled meat into thick slices.
Heat oil in a pan and sauté the onions till slightly brown. Add the carrots, chillie powder, coriander powder, garam masala powder, (½ teaspoon salt if necessary) and about 4 tablespoons of the beef soup / stock and cook till the carrots are soft. Now add the cooked Beef slices, and 4 tablespoons red wine (optional) and the remaining soup/stock to the mashed carrots in the pan. Mix well and simmer on low heat for about 10 minutes. Serve with Bread, steamed vegetables and mash potatoes.

27. BEEF STROGANOFF – ANGLO-INDIAN STYLE

This is an easy recipe for the Anglo-Indian version of Beef Stroganoff that was perfected by me!!!

Serves 6   Time required: About 1 hour 20 mins

Ingredients
1 kg Beef Sirloin cut into cubes
2 medium size onions chopped finely
1 tablespoon chopped garlic
250 grams button mushrooms sliced
2 teaspoons crushed black pepper
2 Bay leaves
2 pieces of cinnamon (about one inch size)
1 cup red wine
3 tablespoons cooking oil
Salt to taste
2 tablespoons Worcestershire sauce
2 tablespoons tomato sauce
1 tablespoon chopped mint
1 tablespoon Dijon Mustard
2 tablespoons flour
½ cup cream

Heat the oil in a suitable pan and fry the chopped onions, garlic, bay leaves and cinnamon for a few minutes till the onions turn light brown. Add the beef, mushrooms, and all the other ingredients and stir fry for a few minutes. Add sufficient water (about 2 or 3 glasses) and cook on low heat till the beef is cooked and the gravy is quite thick. Serve with Buttered Toast or Dinner Rolls and Mash Potatoes.

28. FRIED BEEF SLICES

Serves 6   Time required: 1 hour

Ingredients
1 Kg tender beef sliced thinly into strips
1 teaspoon cumin powder

2 teaspoons chopped garlic
1 teaspoon sugar
2 teaspoons chillie powder
2 teaspoons vinegar
2 cloves
2 one inch pieces of cinnamon
Salt to taste
3 tablespoons Oil

Marinate the meat with all the above ingredients and set aside for 3 or 4 hours. Heat the oil in a suitable pan. Add the marinated meat and sauté till the beef is cooked and crispy. Serve as a side dish with rice and pepper water or Bread

29. MUTTON / LAMB CRUMB CHOPS

Serves 6   Time 1 hour

Ingredients
1 kg tender mutton chops (flatten them by beating)
3 teaspoons ground black pepper / pepper powder
Salt to taste
4 tablespoons bread crumbs
4 tablespoons oil
2 eggs beaten well
2 onions chopped finely
3 teaspoons chopped mint

Marinate the mutton / Lamb chops with the salt, pepper powder and mint over night or for at least 4 to 5 hours.
Heat the oil in a flat frying pan. Dip the chops one at a time in the beaten egg. Top with the chopped onions and cover well with bread crumbs. Shallow fry the chops on both sides in the hot oil on low heat. Fry each side till golden brown. Serve with wedges of lime and Tomato Sauce and Bread.

30. MUTTON CURRY / LAMB CURRY

Serves 6   Time required: 1 hour

Ingredients
1kg mutton or lamb cut into medium pieces
3 tablespoons oil
2 large onions chopped finely
1 tablespoon ginger garlic paste
½ teaspoon turmeric powder
2 teaspoons chillie powder
1 teaspoon cumin powder
1 teaspoon coriander powder
2 tomatoes chopped
Salt to taste
2 tablespoons chopped coriander leaves
2 medium size potatoes peeled and cut into quarters

Heat the oil in a suitable pan and sauté the onions till golden brown. Add the mutton / lamb pieces, potatoes, and all the other ingredients and mix well. Fry for a few more minutes till the tomatoes turn to pulp and the oil separates from the mixture. Add sufficient water and cook till the mutton / lamb is cooked and till the gravy is thick. (Alternately pressure cook for 10 to 15 minutes). Serve with steamed rice.

31. MUTTON FRY (LAMB FRY)

Serves 6   Time required: 45 minutes

Ingredients
1 kg lamb or mutton from the thigh portion cut into medium pieces
1 big tomato chopped
2 large onions sliced finely
2 green chilies sliced lengthwise
1 teaspoon ginger garlic paste
2 tablespoons oil
1 teaspoon chillie powder

½ teaspoon turmeric powder
Salt to taste
2 potatoes boiled. Peeled and cut into quarters

Wash the mutton / lamb and cook it together with the tomato, turmeric and Salt. Let a little soup remain. Now add the chillie powder, green chilies, sliced onions and ginger garlic paste and cook on low heat till all the soup dries up. Add the oil and keep on frying on low heat till the meat turns brown. Add the potatoes and mix gently so that the gravy coats the potatoes. Serve as a side dish with Bread or Rice and Dhal or Pepper Water

32. MUTTON KORMA

Serves 6   Time required: 45 minutes

Ingredients
½ kg good mutton or lamb cut into medium pieces
2 big tomatoes pureed
1 cup curds (yogurt)
1 teaspoon all spice powder (garam masala powder)
½ cup coconut paste
2 tablespoons ginger garlic paste
1 tablespoon chopped mint leaves
2 teaspoons chillie powder
Salt to taste
3 tablespoons oil
2 potatoes pealed and each cut into 8 pieces

Heat oil in a pan and add the ginger garlic paste. Fry for some time. Add the meat and the chillie powder and mix well. Keep frying on low heat for some more time. Now add the tomatoes, curds, salt, mint leaves, potatoes, spice powder / garam masala powder and the coconut and mix well. Add sufficient water and cook till the meat is done and the gravy is thick. (Alternately pressure cook for 12 to 15 minutes).
Serve hot with steamed rice or any Indian Bread.

33. MUTTON GRAVY CHOPS

Tender mutton / lamb Chops are simmered in a thick gravy of coconut, mint and coriander leaves

Serves 6   Time required: 45 minutes

Ingredients
½ kg Mutton or Lamb Chops or steaks
2 teaspoons ginger garlic paste
4 green chilies
3 tablespoons coriander leaves
2 tablespoons mint leaves
1 teaspoon cumin seeds
3 cloves
A one inch piece of Cinnamon bark
½ teaspoon turmeric powder
Salt to taste
3 tablespoons oil
3 potatoes pealed washed and cut into quarters
2 onions sliced finely
½ cup coconut paste

Grind the green chilies, coriander leaves, mint, coconut, cinnamon, cloves, cardamoms and cumin seeds to a smooth paste in a blender. Heat oil in a pressure cooker and fry the onions till golden brown. Add the meat, ginger garlic paste and turmeric powder and fry for some time. Now add the ground masala and salt and mix well with the meat. Keep frying on low heat till the oil separates from the mixture. Add the potatoes and sufficient water and pressure cook for 15 minutes. Serve hot. This curry is good with ghee rice or Palau rice.

34. MUTTON / LAMB MASALA CHOPS

Serves 6   Time required: 1 hour

Ingredients
½ kg good mutton / lamb chops
2 teaspoons ginger garlic paste

2 tablespoons vinegar
2 large onions sliced fine
2 or 3 green chilies sliced lengthwise
3 tablespoons oil
2 teaspoons chillie powder
1 teaspoon ground black pepper / pepper powder
Salt to taste
1 teaspoon cumin powder
1 teaspoon coriander powder

Wash the chops and marinate them with the ginger and garlic paste, pepper powder, chillie powder, vinegar, cumin powder, coriander powder and salt for about 30 minutes.

Heat oil in a large pan and sauté the onions and green chilies for a few minutes. Add the marinated chops and mix well. Simmer for a few minutes. Add sufficient water and cook on low heat till the chops are done and the gravy dries up. Garnish with onion rings. Serve with bread or chapattis.

Note: You could use the same recipe for Beef or Veal Chops if desired.

35. PEPPER MUTTON / LAMB CHOPS

Serves   Time required: 1 hour

Ingredients
½ kg rack of mutton or lamb chops (flatten them slightly)
2 large onions sliced fine
2 or 3 green chilies sliced lengthwise
3 tablespoons oil
2 teaspoons ground black pepper / black pepper powder
3 potatoes peeled and halved

Wash the chops and marinate them with the pepper powder, and salt for about 30 minutes. Heat oil in a large pan and sauté the onions and green chilies for a few minutes. Add the marinated chops and mix well.

Simmer for a few minutes till the chops get firm. Add sufficient water and the potatoes and cook till the chops are done and the gravy dries up. Garnish the rack with onion rings. Serve with bread and steamed vegetables.

36. DOUBLE ONIONS MUTTON CURRY (MUTTON DOPIAZA)

*Dopiaza Mutton or Chicken Dishes were very popular in Anglo-Indian homes in Calcutta and across Bengal. **Do Piaza** when translated literally means **"two onions,"**. This means that the Do Piaza Curry is prepared with almost double the quantity of onions as compared to a normal Meat or chicken curry. In a Dopiaza Curry, half the quantity of the onions are fried and the remaining onions are later added raw to the curry. The prominent flavour of onions gives a slight sweet taste to the curry.*

Serves 6   Time required: 1 hour

Ingredients
½ kg Mutton
4 large onions sliced
2 bay leaves
2 teaspoon chillie powder
1 teaspoon ginger garlic paste
1 teaspoon coriander powder
1 teaspoon all spice powder or garam masala powder
2 tablespoons lime juice
Salt to taste
3 tablespoons oil
2 dry Red chillies broken into bits
2 cloves
2 cardamoms
2 one pieces of cinnamon
2 tablespoon curds / yoghurt

Marinate the mutton with chillie powder, ginger garlic paste, coriander powder, spice powder / garam masala powder and salt and keep aside for 1 hour. Heat the oil in a suitable pan or pressure cooker and sauté half of the onions along with the Bay leaves, Red chillies, cloves, cinnamon and cardamom. Add the marinated meat and mix well. Simmer on low heat for about 5 minutes. Add the remaining sliced onions, curds and 2 glasses of water and mix well. Cook covered on low heat for 1 hour (or pressure cook for 15 minutes) till the mutton is tender and the gravy is quite thick. Garnish with Chopped Coriander leaves. Serve with Rice or chapattis.

Note: Beef or Chicken can also be used instead.

37. SLOW COOKED MUTTON / LAMB STEW

Serves 6   Time required: approx 1 hour

Ingredients
¾ kg tender Mutton or lamb cut into medium size pieces
2 onions chopped finely
1 teaspoon chillie powder
1 teaspoon cumin Powder
1 tablespoon ginger garlic paste
3 tablespoons chopped coriander leaves
1 tablespoon chopped mint leaves
3 green chillies
4 cloves
8 black pepper corns
2 one inch pieces cinnamon
2 bay leaves
1 cup cream or yogurt
Salt to taste
3 tablespoons oil

Marinate the meat with chillie powder, cumin powder, ginger garlic paste, coriander leaves, mint, green chillies, salt and yogurt / cream and leave in the fridge for about 6 hours or overnight.

Heat oil in a suitable thick bottomed pan and add the onions, cloves, bay leaves, cinnamon, and pepper corns and sauté for 2 minutes. Add the marinated meat. Stir fry for about 5 to 7 minutes till the pieces become firm and the oil separates from the mixture. Close the pan with a tight fitting lid. Add 2 cups of water and cook on low heat without opening the pan for about 30 minutes or till the meat is cooked and the gravy is a quite thick. Garnish with chopped Coriander leaves. Serve with dinner Rolls or Bread and steamed vegetables.

Note: You could substitute the Mutton or lamb with beef, veal, chicken, duck etc

38. BRAISED MUTTON / LAMB SHANKS
A shank is the portion of meat around the tibia or shin of the sheep or goat as the case may be. Lamb shanks are usually cooked or braised whole

Serves 6   Time required: approx 1 hour

Ingredients
6 Mutton / Lamb shanks
2 onions sliced
1 teaspoon coriander powder
1 teaspoon cumin powder
1 teaspoon chillie powder
1 teaspoon ground pepper
2 tablespoons vinegar
2 tablespoons tomato sauce or tomato puree
3 tablespoons Oil
Salt to taste

Marinate the mutton / lamb shanks with all the above ingredients and leave in the refrigerator overnight. Transfer to a suitable pan and cook closed on high heat for a couple of minutes. Lower the heat and simmer till the shanks are tender and soft. Serve with either Rice, Chapattis or bread

----

B. CHICKEN

1. CHICKEN JALFRAZIE
Jalfrazie is a sautéd dish, which can be prepared with meat, poultry, sea food etc. The word "Jalfrazie" came from 2 words: "Jal" meaning "spicy or pungent" and "Frazie" meaning "Fried". As in the case of almost all of our cuisine, which started out as insipid concoctions, in the days of the British Raj, the original "Jal Frezie" was bland and tasteless. The Colonial servants would fry up the leftover Christmas Turkey and Chicken Roasts with some pepper, chillies, etc., for Breakfast the next day. Over the years many more ingredients and spices were added to this dish to make it as spicy and delicious as it is today and it has become synonymous with the cuisine of the Anglo-Indians of West Bengal.

Serves 6   Time required: 1 hour

Ingredients
1 kg Boneless Chicken cut into cubes
1 teaspoon cumin seeds
3 dry red chillies broken into bits
2 teaspoons ginger garlic paste
2 tomatoes chopped
2 onions sliced finely
2 capsicums chopped into medium sized pieces
2 green chillies chopped
1 teaspoon spice powder or garam masala powder
1 teaspoon peppercorns
3 tablespoons oil
Salt to taste

Heat oil in a suitable pan and add the cumin seeds. When they begin to splutter add the dry red chillies, onions and pepper corns and fry till golden brown. Add the chicken and sauté for a few minutes till it changes colour. Now add all the other ingredients and stir well. Simmer on low heat till the chicken is tender and the gravy is quite thick. Serve with pepper water and rice or chapattis, bread, dinner rolls, etc.

2. CHICKEN IN COCONUT GRAVY

In the olden days this dish was prepared with home grown country fowls in thick coconut gravy. It was left to simmer for many hours over a firewood oven. However, I have simplified the recipe and one could use any tender chicken instead of the country fowl.

Serves 6   Time required: 45 minutes

Ingredients
1 Country Fowl or Farm Chicken (weighing around 1.50 kg)
cut into medium size pieces
3 onions chopped finely
2 large tomatoes chopped
2 teaspoons ginger garlic paste
1 teaspoon coriander powder
1 teaspoon turmeric powder
½ cup grated coconut
2 small pieces cinamon bark
3 cloves
2 cardamoms
Salt to taste
2 teaspoons chopped coriander leaves
2 teaspoons chopped mint leaves
3 tablespoons oil
2 teaspoons chillie powder
2 tablespoons curds

Grind the coconut, cinamon, cloves, cardamom and half the onions to a smooth paste.
Heat oil in a pan and fry the remaining onions till golden brown. Add the ground paste and fry for about 5 minutes on low heat. Add the chillie powder, ginger garlic paste, spice powder, coriander powder, turmeric powder and tomatoes and keep frying till the tomatoes are reduced to pulp. Now add the chicken and curds and mix well. Add salt, mint and coriander leaves and 3 cups of water and simmer till the chicken is cooked and gravy is thick. Serve hot with rice or chapattis.

3. CHICKEN PEPPER FRY

Serves 6   Time required: 30 minutes

Ingredients
1 kg chicken cut into medium size pieces
3 large onions sliced finely
2 teaspoons ground black pepper / pepper powder
½ teaspoon turmeric powder (optional)
2 tablespoons oil
Salt to taste

Heat oil in a pan and fry the onions lightly. Add the chicken and mix in the pepper powder, turmeric powder and salt. Stir fry for about 2 minutes till the chicken pieces get firm. Add ½ a cup of water and cook on low heat till the chicken is tender and semi dry. Simmer for 10 more minutes, stirring occasionally, till the chicken gets a good shiny colour. Serve as a Side dish or as a snack.

Alternately, the chicken can be par boiled with a little water and then added to the sautéed onions and pepper.

4. HURRY-BURRY CHICKEN CURRY
(JALDHI-JALDHI CHICKEN CURRY)
*Anglo-Indian English is a fascinating creative combination of old English expressions from colonial times, ungrammatical sentence constructions and direct translations from native Indian languages such as Tamil, Hindi etc, besides words borrowed from other colonial languages. The simplification of the Queen's English and the use of vernacular words and syntax and direct translation of phrases, increased the user-friendliness of the language. Hurry-Burry is one such term which denotes their fondness for rhyming alliterative words. Just as the name implies, this delicious **Chicken Curry can be made in a hurry.** However, don't be too much in haste to get it done as your 'hurry-burry' can spoil the Curry!*

Serves 6   Time required: 30 Minutes

Ingredients
1 kg chicken jointed and cut into medium size pieces
2 tomatoes chopped finely
2 large onions chopped
½ teaspoon turmeric powder
2 or 3 teaspoons chillie powder
1 teaspoon cumin powder
1 teaspoon coriander powder
3 cloves
2 small pieces of cinamon
2 teaspoons ginger garlic paste
3 tablespoons oil
Salt to taste
2 tablespoons vinegar
2 tablespoons chopped coriander leaves

Make a thick paste with the turmeric powder, chillie powder, cumin powder, coriander powder, ginger garlic paste, salt and vinegar. Apply this paste on the chicken and keep aside.
Meanwhile heat oil in a pan and add the onions, cinamon and cloves, Fry till golden brown. Now add the marinated chicken and chopped tomatoes, and fry for some time till the oil separates from the mixture. Add sufficient water and cook till the chicken is done and the gravy is thick. Garnish with chopped coriander leaves. Serve with rice or any Indian Bread.

5. RED MASALA CHICKEN CURRY
This is an old Colonial Dish conceived and perfected by the cooks / khansamas in the Travellers Bungalows / Guest Houses of yore. The Dak Bungalow Red Masala Chicken Curry is still prepared by the cooks in the present day Inspection / Travellers' Bungalows and Government Guest Houses as the 'Laal Murgi Curry'!

Serves 6   Time required: 45 minutes

Ingredients:
1 Kg chicken cut into medium size pieces
1 teaspoon all spice powder or garam masala powder
3 teaspoons chopped garlic

2 teaspoon chillie powder
1 teaspoon coriander powder
3 onions sliced
Salt to taste
2 green chillies
½ teaspoon turmeric powder
½ teaspoon pepper powder
2 tablespoons oil
1 tablespoon lime juice
½ cup curds / yogurt

Mix all the ingredients mentioned above with the chicken in a suitable pan and set it aside for about 1 hour. Place the pan on medium heat and cook closed for about 5 to 6 minutes. Lower the heat and mix well. Add enough water and then simmer on low heat till the chicken is cooked and the gravy thickens. Serve with rice or chapattis.

6. SOUTH STYLE ANGLO-INDIAN CHICKEN VINDALOO

Serves 6   Time required: 45 minutes

Ingredients
1 kg chicken jointed and cut into medium pieces
3 big tomatoes pureed
2 big onions chopped
3 medium potatoes peeled and cut into quarters
3 tablespoons oil
Salt to taste
1 teaspoon mustard powder or paste
2 teaspoons chillie powder
1 teaspoon cumin powder
2 teaspoons garlic paste
½ cup vinegar
½ teaspoon turmeric powder

Heat oil in a suitable pan or pressure cooker and fry the onions till golden brown. Add the garlic paste and fry well. Add the chicken, chillie powder, turmeric powder, cumin powder, mustard powder and fry well on medium heat, till the oil separates from the mixture. Add the tomato puree and salt and fry for some more time. Now, add the potatoes and vinegar and mix well. Add more water depending on how much gravy is required and cook till done.

(If cooking in a pressure cooker, turn off the heat after 2 or 3 whistles). The dish should be a lovely red colour. Serve with hoppers, bread, rice or chapattis.

7. 'TWICE THE ONIONS' CHICKEN CURRY (CHICKEN DO PIAZZA)

Serves 6   Time required: 1 hour

Ingredients
1 medium sized chicken weighing around 1 kg cut into medium size pieces
4 large onions sliced
2 bay leaves
2 teaspoon chillie powder
2 teaspoons ginger garlic paste
1 teaspoons coriander powder
1 teaspoon all spice powder or garam masala powder
Salt to taste
3 tablespoons oil
2 dry Red chillies broken into bits
2 cloves
1 piece cinnamon
2 tablespoon curds / yoghurt (optional)

Marinate the chicken with chillie powder, ginger garlic paste, coriander powder, all spice powder / garam masala powder, curds / yogurt and salt and keep aside for 1 hour.

Heat the oil in a suitable pan or pressure cooker and sauté half of the onions along with the Bay leaves, Red chillies, cloves and cinnamon. Add the marinated chicken and mix well. Simmer on low heat for about 5 minutes. Add the remaining sliced onions and 1 cup of water and cook covered on low heat for about 25 to 30 minutes (stirring occasionally), till the chicken is tender. Garnish with Chopped Coriander leaves. Serve with Rice or chapattis.

8. COUNTRY CAPTAIN CHICKEN

Serves 6   Time required: 40 minutes

Ingredients:
1 kg chicken cut into medium size pieces
4 large onions sliced finely
2 teaspoons chillie powder
1 teaspoon turmeric powder
3 tablespoons oil
Salt to taste
2 teaspoons ginger garlic paste
2 small sticks cinnamon
4 cloves
6 or 8 whole pepper corns
2 Dry Red Chillies broken into bits

Heat oil in a pan and fry the onions cinnamon, cloves, red chillie and pepper corns till golden brown. Remove half the fried onions and keep aside. Add the chicken to the pan and mix in the ginger garlic paste and sauté for about 5 minutes on medium heat. Add the chillie powder, turmeric powder, and salt. Mix well and stir fry for a few minutes. Add ½ cup of water and cook till the chicken is tender and the gravy is quite thick. Now add the remaining browned onions and mix well. Simmer for a few more minutes, then, turn off the heat. The gravy should be quite thick so that it coats the pieces of chicken nicely.

Note: This recipe can be adapted to meat as well. Left over Beef or Lamb Roast can be made into a delicious Country Captain Fry or a cold meat curry if desired.

9. CHICKEN DUMPLING STEW

Serves 6   Time required: 45 minutes

Ingredients for the Stew:
1 medium sized chicken washed and jointed into fairly big pieces
2 cups coconut milk
1 teaspoon chopped garlic
1 teaspoon chopped ginger
3 onions sliced
Salt to taste
3 green chillies slit lengthwise
2 small pieces of cinnamon
½ teaspoon turmeric powder
1 teaspoon chillie powder
1 teaspoon ground black pepper / pepper powder
2 tablespoons oil
1 tablespoon chopped mint leaves

Ingredients for the Dumplings,
1 cup of flour
1 teaspoon butter
½ teaspoon salt

To make the Dumplings, mix the flour, butter and salt together with a little water to form a soft dough. Form into small balls and flatten slightly. Keep aside

Heat the oil in a suitable pan and fry the onions, cinnamon, garlic and ginger till the onions turn light brown. Add the chicken and all the above ingredients for the stew and mix well. (Add a little more water if desired). Cook closed on high heat for about 5 to 6 minutes. Lower the heat and add the dumplings to the stew. Simmer for 15 to 20 minutes till the chicken is cooked and the stew is slightly thick. Serve with bread or steamed rice or Hoppers.

10. CHICKEN AND VEGETABLE STEW

Serves 6   Time required: 1 hour

Ingredients
1 chicken weighing around 1 kg cut into medium pieces
3 carrots
4 French beans
2 potatoes peeled
3 green chilies slit lengthwise
1 medium size tomato chopped
1 big onion sliced
2 teaspoons ginger garlic paste
2 cloves,
2 small pieces of cinnamon,
6 or 7 pepper corns
A few mint leaves
Salt to taste
2 tablespoons oil
3 tablespoons coconut milk
2 tablespoons flour

Wash the vegetables and cut into medium size pieces.
Cook the chicken together with the cut vegetables, pepper corns, green chilies, tomato, ginger garlic paste, salt, cinnamon, cloves, mint, coconut, and sufficient water till the chicken is cooked.

Make a thin paste of 2 tablespoons flour with¼ cup of water.
In another pan heat the oil and fry the onions till golden brown. Add the flour paste and fry along with the onions for some time. Add the cooked chicken and vegetables and mix well. Simmer for 5 minutes. Serve hot with bread or hoppers.

11. CHICKEN ALMORTH STEW

Serves 6   Time required: 1 hour and 15 minutes

Ingredients
1 tender Chicken weighing around 1Kg
1 large cabbage cut into 4
3 carrots cut into medium pieces
3 potatoes cut into medium pieces
2 teaspoons salt
2 large onions sliced
3 green chilies slit lengthwise
2 teaspoons ginger garlic paste
2 small pieces cinamon
3 cloves
1 teaspoon chilie powder
2 teaspoons ground black pepper / pepper powder
2 Bay leaves
1 teaspoon cumin powder
1 teaspoon coriander powder
2 tablespoons vinegar
3 tablespoons oil

Chop the chicken into medium size pieces and rub it well with a little salt and vinegar.
Cut the vegetables into medium size pieces. Place the chicken and vegetables together with all the above ingredients in a suitable pan or crock pot. Cover and cook on low heat for about one hour or till the chicken and vegetables are well cooked and gives out a nice aroma. Serve hot with bread.

12. CHICKEN DEVIL FRY
The term 'Devilled' originated during the time of the British Raj in India. The Colonial servants would recycle the leftover Turkey and Chicken Roasts into a hot Fry or Dry Dish with the addition of some hot seasonings or condiments such as pepper, chillies, etc. Hence the term 'Devilled'. This spicy dish tickles the palate with a burst of flavours.

Serves 6   Time required: 45 minutes

Ingredients
1 kg chicken cut into medium size pieces or left over Chicken Roast
3 teaspoons chopped garlic
2 teaspoon chillie powder
3 onions sliced
2 tablespoons tomato sauce or ketchup
Salt to taste
3 green chillies
1 teaspoon pepper powder
1 teaspoon cumin powder
3 tablespoons oil
2 tablespoons vinegar
2 one inch pieces of cinnamon

Fry the onions, cinnamon, green chillies and garlic till the onions turn golden brown. Add the chicken and fry for about 2 or 3 minutes. Now add all the other ingredients and mix well. Fry till the oil separates from the mixture. Add ½ cup of water and mix well. Cover the pan and simmer on low heat till the chicken is cooked and the gravy is very thick.
Serve as a side dish with dhal and rice or Pepper Water and rice. It could also be served as a starter or appetizer.

13. SIMPLE CHICKEN DRY FRY
This is a very simple but tasty Chicken Fry. The butter or ghee that is added at the end together with fried curry leaves and raw Onion Rings enhance the taste of the dish.

Serves 6   Time required: 45 minutes

Ingredients
1 medium sized chicken washed and cut into fairly big pieces
2 teaspoons ginger garlic paste
2 onions ground into a paste
Salt to taste
1 teaspoon chillie powder
1 teaspoon cumin powder

2 tablespoons vinegar
2 tablespoons oil

To Garnish
1 tablespoon butter
8 or 10 curry leaves fried in a little butter
1 large onion cut into thin rings

Marinate the chicken with all the ingredients mentioned above for an hour (except the ingredients for garnish).
Transfer to a suitable pan and cook on low heat till the chicken is tender and semi-dry. Mix in a tablespoon of butter and let the dish rest for about 15 minutes before serving. Garnish with fried curry leaves and raw onion rings.
Serve as a side dish with Pepper Water and Rice or Dhal and Rice or a snack or appetizer at a party.

Note: Instead of frying t he chicken, it could be grilled in an oven. Arrange the pieces on a flat dish and grill for about half an hour in a hot oven.

14. TAMARIND CHICKEN CURRY (TANGY CHICKEN CURRY)

Serves 6   Time required: 45 minutes

Ingredients:
1kg chicken cut into medium size pieces
2 big onions sliced
½ teaspoon coriander powder
2 teaspoons chillie powder
1teaspoon ginger garlic paste
Salt to taste
2 tablespoons oil
½ cup thick tamarind juice
3 green chillies slit lengthwise.

Wash the chicken and mix it with the ginger garlic paste, salt, coriander powder and the chillie powder. Heat oil in a pan and fry the onions till golden brown. Add the chicken and mix well. Fry for a few minutes. Add sufficient water and cook on medium heat till the chicken is tender. Add the thick tamarind juice and mix well. Keep frying till the gravy is thick and dark brown. Garnish with slit green chillies. Let the curry stand for half an hour before serving to draw in all the flavours. Serve with steamed rice or chappatis.

15. MADRAS CHICKEN CURRY

Serves 6   Time required: 25 minutes

Ingredients
1 kg chicken cut into medium size pieces
3 onions sliced finely
2 tomatoes chopped finely
½ teaspoon turmeric powder
3 tablespoons oil
2 teaspoons chillie powder
1 teaspoon coriander powder
1 teaspoon cumin powder
2 teaspoons chopped mint or parsley
2 teaspoon chopped coriander leaves
½ teaspoon cinamon powder
½ teaspoon nutmeg powder (optional)
3 tablespoons coconut milk
Salt to taste

Mix the chicken with the salt, chillie powder, turmeric powder, coriander powder, cumin powder, cinamon powder and nutmeg powder for about 10 minutes.
Meanwhile heat the oil in a pan and sauté the onions to golden brown. Toss in the marinated chicken pieces, chopped tomatoes and the mint / parsley and mix well. Fry on low heat till the oil separates from the mixture. Add the coconut milk and about 2 cups of water and mix well. Close the pan with a lid and cook on low heat for about 20 minutes till the chicken is cooked. Garnish with the chopped coriander leaves.
Serve with Steamed Rice or bread

16. CRUMB FRIED CHICKEN

Serves 6   Time required: 1 hour

Ingredients
6 chicken breasts
3 teaspoons pepper powder
2 teaspoons chopped mint
Salt to taste
2 tablespoons butter
3 tablespoons oil
5 tablespoons lime juice or vinegar
3 tablespoons corn flour

Beat each chicken breast with a mallet or cleaver and then flatten with a rolling pin. Marinate the flattened chicken with the pepper powder, mint, salt, lime juice / vinegar, corn flour and one tablespoon butter and keep aside for 15 minutes.

Heat a little oil in a nonstick pan and fry the chicken pieces on medium heat till tender. When all the pieces are fried, add 2 tablespoons butter and sauté the chicken for about 5 minutes on low heat. Serve with butter rice or bread.
(Alternately the chicken can be baked in an oven using the same recipe)

17. CHRISTINE'S CHICKEN PEPPER STEAK

Serves 6   Time required: 1 hour

Ingredients
6 Chicken Breasts
1 teaspoon coriander Powder
½ teaspoon turmeric powder
2 teaspoons ground black pepper / black Pepper powder
3 tablespoons Cream or milk
1 teaspoon lime / lemon juice
3 tablespoons oil
Salt to taste

Lightly pound the Chicken Breasts to flatten then marinate them with all the above ingredients for about one hour. Transfer to a suitable Pan. Place the pan on high heat and sear the Chicken Steaks on both sides for about 3 or 4 minutes. Lower the heat and cook till the Chicken is tender and both sides are brown.

Remove on to a serving dish. Add 2 tablespoons butter and a little water to the residue in the pan to make a gravy sauce. Pour this gravy sauce over the Chicken Steaks. Serve with bread and steamed vegetables such as peas, carrot strips and cauliflower or broccoli florets.

18. ROASTED CHICKEN BREASTS

The Chicken Breasts are braised and roasted in a closed pan in this recipe so as that the Chicken breasts are juicy and succulent and not dry.

Serves 6   Time required: 1 hour

Ingredients
6 Chicken Breasts
2 teaspoons lime juice or vinegar
2 teaspoons chopped garlic
4 tablespoons Butter
Salt to taste
2 teaspoons whole pepper corns
2 onions chopped into big chunks

Heat the butter in a suitable pan and add the chicken Breasts and all the other ingredients. Mix well and stir fry on high heat for a few minutes till the chicken changes colour. Add a little water and simmer on low heat till the chicken is tender and the water dries up. Keep frying on low heat for a few more minutes till the chicken pieces are nicely browned. Serve with Mashed Potatoes, steamed vegetables and Bread.

19. NANA'S SLOW ROASTED CHICKEN AND POTATOES

Slow roasting is a proven method of keeping the Chicken Roast juicy and moist. The Potatoes or turnips that are added, while roasting the chicken, gives them a wonderful roasted flavor as well. Moreover, the potatoes absorb any extra salt in the roast.

Serves 6   Time required: 1 hour

Ingredients
1 whole tender chicken medium size
Salt to taste
2 teaspoons ground black pepper powder
2 tablespoons oil or butter
3 large potatoes or turnips rinsed well

Marinate the chicken with the salt and pepper for about 15 to 20 minutes. Heat oil or ghee in a thick -bottomed pan, and add the whole chicken. Turn the chicken from side to side and fry for about for about 5 minutes. Add the potatoes / turnips. Add 2 cups of water. Cover the pan with a tight lid and cook over low heat turning the chicken occasionally till the chicken is cooked and all the stock is absorbed. Remove the potatoes / turnips and keep aside.
Continue to cook on low heat till the chicken is roasted to a lovely golden brown. Remove on to a serving dish.
Put back the potatoes / turnips into the same pan and sprinkle a little water on the residue in the pan. Mix this with the potatoes / turnips. Remove the Roasted potatoes / turnips and place along with the Chicken Roast. Serve with steamed vegetables and bread or dinner rolls.
Note: The chicken could also be roasted in an oven following the same procedures.

20. CHICKEN POTATO CHOPS (CHICKEN POTATO CUTLETS)

Serves 6   Time required: 1 hour

Ingredients
2 cups boiled and shredded chicken
3 potatoes boiled and mashed
4 tablespoons breadcrumbs
3 eggs beaten
1 tablespoon chopped mint or parsley
Salt to taste
1 teaspoon ground black pepper / pepper powder
4 tablespoons oil

Mix the boiled and shredded chicken with the pepper powder, salt and chopped mint. Form the mashed potatoes into even sized balls. Make a depression in the center and fill with the shredded chicken. Flatten each ball to form an oval shaped chop / cutlet. Dip each cutlet /chop in the beaten egg then roll in the breadcrumbs. Heat oil in a flat pan and shallow fry the chops / cutlets on low heat till golden brown on both sides.

Serve with mint sauce or tomato sauce.

21. CHICKEN LIVER PEPPER FRY

Serves 6   Time required: 45 minutes

Ingredients
½ kg chicken livers cut into pieces
2 large onions sliced finely
2 or 3 teaspoons ground black pepper / pepper powder
2 green chillies slit
Salt to taste
3 tablespoons oil

Rinse the chicken gizzards and livers well. Boil them with a little water and salt till well cooked.

Heat oil in a pan and fry the onions till golden brown. Add the cooked gizzards and liver together with the slit green chillies, pepper powder and salt and keep frying on low heat till dry and brown. Serve as a snack or side dish with bread or rice

22. SIMPLE DUCK VINDALOO

Serves 6   Time required:1 hour

Ingredients
1 medium size duck jointed into medium size pieces
3 big tomatoes pureed
2 big onions chopped
3 tablespoons oil

Salt to taste
1 teaspoon mustard powdered
3 teaspoons chillie powder
2 teaspoons cumin powder
1 teaspoon ground black pepper / pepper powder
3 teaspoons ginger garlic paste
½ cup vinegar
½ teaspoon turmeric powder

Heat oil in a suitable pan or pressure cooker and fry the onions till golden brown. Add the duck and the ginger garlic paste and fry well till the pieces turn firm. Add the chillie powder, turmeric powder, cumin powder, mustard powder, pepper powder and a little water and fry well till the oil separates from the mixture. Now add the tomato puree and salt and fry for some more time. Add the vinegar and mix well. Add sufficient water depending on how much gravy is required. Cover the pan and cook on low heat till the duck is tender.
(If cooking in a pressure cooker, turn off the heat after 9 or 10 whistles).
Serve with steamed rice or bread.

23. DUCK STEW IN COCONUT MILK

Serves 6   Time required:1 hour and 15 minutes

Ingredients
1 tender duck cut into medium size pieces
3 big onions sliced finely
2 tomatoes chopped into big chunks
8 to 10 green chilies sliced lengthwise
2 teaspoons ginger garlic paste
1cup thick coconut milk
1 teaspoon turmeric powder
1 teaspoon ground black pepper /pepper powder
3 tablespoons oil
2 tablespoons vinegar
Salt to taste

Wash the duck well and rub all over with the vinegar and turmeric powder. Heat oil in a pressure cooker or a suitable pan and lightly fry the pieces of duck. When the pieces turn light brown add all the other ingredients to it. Mix well so that all the pieces get covered. Add about 2 or 3 cups of water and mix well. Cook on medium heat till the duck is cooked and the gravy thickens.
(If cooking in a pressure cooker, turn off the heat after 9 or 10 whistles).
Serve with hoppers or Steamed rice

24. DUCK DEVIL FRY

Serves 6   Time required: 45 minutes

Ingredients:
1 kg duck cut into medium size pieces or left over Duck Roast
3 teaspoons chopped garlic
2 teaspoon chillie powder
3 onions sliced
1 tomato chopped finely
2 tablespoons tomato sauce or ketchup
Salt to taste
3 green chillies
½ teaspoon turmeric powder
1 teaspoon ground black pepper / pepper powder
1 teaspoon cumin powder
3 tablespoons oil
2 tablespoons vinegar
2 tablespoons Worcestershire sauce or soya sauce
2 or 3 pieces of cinnamon about ½ inch long

Boil the duck with 2 glasses of water and some salt in a pressure cooker. Fry the onions, cinnamon, green chillies and garlic till the onions turn golden brown. Add all the other ingredients and fry well for a couple of minutes. Now add the cooked duck with the left over stock and continue frying on medium heat till most of the gravy dries up.
Serve as a side dish with dhal and rice or Pepper Water and rice. It could also be served as a starter or appetizer

25. NANA'S SPECIAL DUCK ROAST

Serves 6   Time required: 1 hour

Ingredients
1 whole duck with the skin
2 or 3 pods of garlic chopped very finely
3 teaspoons ground black pepper / pepper powder
1 teaspoon chillie powder
½ teaspoon turmeric powder
Salt to taste
3 dried red chillies
2 teaspoons Tomato sauce
2 teaspoons vinegar
3 tablespoons oil
3 large potatoes peeled

Heat the oil in a big Pan or Pressure Cooker and add the whole duck. Sear the duck on high heat for about 3 minutes, turning on all sides till it changes colour. Add all the other ingredients and about 4 glasses of water and simmer till tender. Strain away any excess soup and keep aside. Remove the potatoes. Add 2 tablespoons of oil or ghee and continue to simmer on low heat till the duck is nicely roasted. Slice and arrange on a serving platter with the potatoes

Pour the remaining soup back into the pan and mix in 2 tablespoons of flour. Cook till the gravy thickens, stirring all the time. Spoon this gravy on top of the slices of the Duck Roast. Pour the remaining gravy on the side of the platter along with the Roast potatoes. Alternatively the duck could be cooked in a pressure cooker till soft and then browned in a pan

----

C. PORK
(Any Pork Cut as per one's choice could be used for preparing these dishes)

1. SIMPLE PORK CURRY

Serves 6   Time required: 45 minutes

Ingredients
1 kg pork (belly portion) with some fat and lard, cut into medium pieces
2 big onions slices finely
2 big tomatoes pureed
1 teaspoon cumin powder
½ teaspoon turmeric powder
2 teaspoons chillie powder
1 teaspoon coriander powder
1 tablespoon ginger garlic paste
3 tablespoons vinegar
2 tablespoons oil
2 tomatoes chopped finely
2 tablespoons chopped coriander leaves
Salt to taste

Marinate the pork for about one hour with all the above ingredients. Transfer to a suitable pan or pressure cooker and keep frying on medium heat for some time till the oil separates from the mixture. Now add sufficient water depending on how much gravy is required and cook till the pork is well cooked. If cooking in a pressure cooker, turn off heat after 7 or 8 whistles.
Serve hot with hoppers, rice or bread.

2. PORK BHOONIE (PORK COOKED WITH DILL LEAVES)
Pork Bhuni is an old Anglo-Indian Dish that is still popular in Calcutta and West Bengal especially in the hills of Darjeeling. The term Bhooni, or Bhuni means 'to Fry' and comes from the Hindi Word 'Bhuna'. In this dish the Pork is cooked along with fresh Dil Leaves and Potatoes and then simmered till done. The almost dry coating consistency of the gravy

that remains on the pork together with the flavour of Fresh Dil leaves makes this Pork Dish unique.

Serves 6   Time required: 45 minutes

Ingredients
1 kg Pork loin with less fat cut into medium pieces
1 teaspoon ginger garlic paste
½ teaspoon turmeric powder
2 teaspoon chillie powder
2 green chillies sliced lengthwise
3 onions sliced finely
1 cup chopped fresh Dill leaves (or use fenugreek /
methi leaves if desired)
Salt to taste
3 Potatoes peeled and cut into quarters
3 tablespoons oil

Heat oil in a pan and fry the onions till golden brown. Add the ginger and garlic paste and sauté for a few more minutes. Add the pork, chillie powder, turmeric powder, green chillies, and Dil leaves and mix well. Stir fry for a few minutes till the meat becomes firm and the leaves shrivel up. Add the potatoes and sufficient water and simmer on low heat till the pork and potatoes are tender.

3. SOUTH STYLE ANGLO-INDIAN PORK VINDALOO

Serves 6   Time required: 45 minutes

Ingredients
1 kg pork loin cut into medium size pieces
3 potatoes peeled and cut into halves
3 large onions sliced finely
2 teaspoons chillie powder
1 teaspoon turmeric powder
2 teaspoons cumin powder
2 tablespoons oil
Salt to taste

2 tablespoons ginger garlic paste
2 small sticks cinnamon
4 cloves
3 tablespoons vinegar

Boil the pork and potatoes with a little salt and sufficient water till tender. Remove and keep aside.
Heat oil in a pan and fry the onions, cinamon and cloves till light brown. Add the ginger garlic paste and sauté for about 5 minutes on medium heat. Add the chillie powder, turmeric powder, cumin powder, vinegar and salt. Fry for a couple of minutes. Now add the cooked pork and potatoes along with the remaining soup and simmer for about 10 minutes till the gravy is sufficiently thick. Serve with bread or rice.

4. MAMA'S SPECIAL TANGY PORK CURRY (PORK IN TAMARIND SAUCE)

Serves 6   Time required: 45 minutes

Ingredients
1 kg pork loin with the fat and lard cut into medium pieces
3 big onions slices finely
3 big tomatoes pureed or chopped finely
1 teaspoon cumin powder
2 teaspoons coriander powder
½ teaspoon turmeric powder
1 teaspoon mustard seeds
3 teaspoons chillie powder
8 or 10 curry leaves
3 teaspoons ginger garlic paste
1 cup tamarind juice extracted from a small ball of tamarind or ½ teaspoon tamarind concentrate
2 tablespoons oil
Salt to taste

Make a powder with 3 Cardamoms, 3 cloves, 2 sticks cinnamon and 2 teaspoons aniseeds or saunf

Heat oil in a pan and add the mustard seeds. When they begin to crackle add the curry leaves and onions and fry till golden brown. Now add the chillie powder, cumin powder, turmeric powder, coriander powder, the powdered spices and ginger garlic paste and fry for some time with a little water. Add the pork, salt and the tomato puree and keep frying for some time till the oil separates from the mixture. Add the tamarind juice and a little more water and cook for about 25 to 30 minutes on low heat till the pork is cooked. Serve hot with rice or bread. (If cooking in a pressure cooker turn off after 6 or 8 whistles)

5. PAPA PAT'S PORK CHOPS

Serves 6   Time required: 1 hour

½ kg good pork chops (rib chops)
2 teaspoons ginger garlic paste
2 tablespoons vinegar
2 large onions sliced finely
2 or 3 green chilies sliced lengthwise
3 tablespoons oil
1 teaspoon chillie powder
1 teaspoon all spice powder or garam masala
1 teaspoon ground black pepper / pepper powder
Salt to taste
3 tablespoons tomato sauce / ketchup

Marinate the pork chops with all the above ingredients for about 5 hours or overnight. Transfer to a suitable pan and cook on high heat for 3 or 4 minutes. Reduce the heat. Add 1 or 2 cups of water and mix well. Cover and cook on low heat till the chops are done and the gravy is quite thick. Garnish with onion rings.

6. ANGLO-INDIAN PORK ROAST

Serves 6   Time required: 1 hour

1 chunk of pork weighing around 2 kg (rump or chump end)
3 whole potatoes peeled

3 whole red chillies broken into bits
1 teaspoon ground black pepper powder
1 teaspoon chillie powder
1 teaspoon pepper corns
3 cloves
3 one inch pieces of cinamon
1 Bay leaf
Salt to taste
2 tablespoons vinegar

Marinate the Pork with the salt, vinegar, chillie powder and ground black pepper. Place in a suitable pan or over proof dish together with the red chillies, peppercorns, spices, bay leaf and fry for 2 or 3 minutes on low heat. Add the whole potatoes and sufficient water. Simmer on low heat turning the pork around till nicely browned on all sides.*(Alternately, the pork roast can be made in an oven)*
Serve with Bread, Potato Mash and steamed vegetables.

7. SIMPLE PORK FRY

Serves 6   Time required: 40 minutes

Ingredients
1 kg pork (belly portion) cut into medium size pieces
3 large onions sliced finely
2 teaspoons chillie powder
½ teaspoon turmeric powder
2 tablespoons oil
Salt to taste
2 tablespoons ginger garlic paste
1 teaspoon cumin powder
2 green chillies
2 tablespoons vinegar

Boil the pork with a little sat and sufficient water till tender.
Heat oil in a pan and fry the onions lightly. Add the ginger garlic paste and sauté for about 2 minutes on medium heat. Add the chillie powder,

cumin powder, green chillies, turmeric powder, and the pork along with the vinegar and cook till the pork is tender and semi dry. This dish could be served as a starter or as a side dish with rice, bread etc

8. PORK DEVIL FRY

Serves 6   Time required: 45 minutes

Ingredients
1 kg Pork (less fat) from the loin portion cut into medium size pieces
2 tablespoons vinegar
1 tablespoon Worcester sauce or Soya Sauce
2 tablespoons Tomato sauce
3 tablespoons oil
3 large onions sliced
2 tablespoons chopped garlic
2 tablespoons chopped ginger
3 dry red chillies broken into bits
2 pieces cinnamon
3 cloves
3 teaspoons chillie powder
½ teaspoon turmeric powder
Salt to taste
3 tablespoons oil

Marinate the pork with the Vinegar, Worcester / Soya Sauce, Tomato Sauce and salt for about 1 hour.
Heat the oil in a pressure Cooker or pan and sauté the onions, red chillies, chopped ginger, chopped garlic, cinnamon and cloves till light brown. Add the marinated pork, chillie powder, turmeric powder, and mix well. Sauté for a few minutes till the pork pieces become firm. Add sufficient water and pressure cook for about 15 to 20 minutes till the pork is cooked. Simmer till almost dry. Serve with Rice, Bread or Chappatis.

9. DEVILLED PORK CHOPS

Serves 6   Time required: 45 minutes

Ingredients
1 kg Pork Chops (Rib chops)
4 green chilies ground to a paste
1 teaspoon mustard powder
2 tablespoons Worcestershire / Soya sauce
2 teaspoon chillie powder
1 teaspoon coriander powder
Salt to taste
2 tablespoons oil
1 teaspoon peppercorns
3 onions sliced finely
2 tablespoons vinegar
3 Potatoes boiled and cut into halves

Marinate the chops with all the above ingredients (except the boiled potatoes) for about one hour. Transfer to a suitable pan or pressure cooker. Cook on high heat for about 5 minutes stirring occasionally. Add 2 cups water and simmer on low heat till the chops are tender and the gravy is thick. Add the Boiled Potatoes and mix once. Serve with Rice or bread.

10. PEPPER PORK SPARE RIBS

Serves 6   Time required: 45 minutes

Ingredients
1 kg Pork Spare Ribs
1 teaspoon Coriander Powder
2 teaspoons ground black pepper
2 teaspoons finely chopped garlic
2 tablespoons oil
Salt to taste
1 teaspoon chillie Powder (as per choice for pungency)

2 tablespoons vinegar
3 onions finely chopped

Marinate the Pork Spare Ribs with the coriander powder, pepper powder, chillie powder, vinegar and salt for one hour.
Heat the oil in a pan and sauté the onions and chopped garlic till golden brown. Add the marinated Pork Spare Ribs and mix well. Add sufficient water and cook till tender. Serve with rice or Bread.
This could also be served as a snack or a starter at parties.

11. PORK BUFFAD

Serves 6   Time required: 45 minutes

Ingredients
1 kg boneless Pork Loin cut into medium pieces
3 large onions sliced finely
2 tablespoons ginger garlic paste
2 tablespoons oil
2 one inch pieces of cinnamon
6 or 7 cloves
4 tablespoons vinegar
1 teaspoon ground black pepper / pepper powder
3 teaspoons chillie powder
1 teaspoon cumin powder
2 teaspoons coriander powder
2 bay leaves
Salt to taste

Mix the pork with all the above ingredients and leave aside for one hour. Transfer to a suitable pan or pressure cooker and fry first on medium heat for about 3 or 4 minutes. Reduce heat, and add sufficient water. Simmer on low heat till the pork is tender. If cooking in a pressure cooker, turn off heat after 10 or 12 whistles.
Serve with rice or bread

12. PORK CHILLIE FRY

Serves 6   Time required: 45 minutes

lingredients:
1 kg Pork (any cut) without the lard cut into small pieces
3 large onions sliced finely
2 medium size capsicums / green peppers sliced thinly (optional)
8 peppercorns
1 teaspoon chopped ginger
1 teaspoon chopped garlic
6 green chillies sliced lengthwise
Salt to taste
3 tablespoons oil

Boil the Pork in 1 cup of water with a little salt and the peppercorns till tender Heat oil in a pan and fry the onions ginger and garlic till golden brown. Add the slit green chillies and sliced capsicum and sauté for a few minutes. Add the boiled pork and a little more salt if necessary and simmer till semi dry. Serve with rice or bread or as a starter at a party.

13. PORK PEPPER FRY

Serves 6   Time required: 1 hour

Ingredients
1 kg tender pork (belly portion) cut into cubes
2 green chillies sliced
3 onions sliced finely
2 teaspoons chopped garlic
1 teaspoon chopped ginger
3 or 4 teaspoons ground black pepper / pepper powder
8 or 10 curry leaves (optional)
Salt to taste

Cook the pork with a little salt and a pinch of turmeric in sufficient water till tender. Strain the soup and keep aside.

Heat the oil in a pan and sauté the onions, ginger, garlic, curry leaves and green chillies till slightly brown. Add the cooked pork, pepper powder, and salt and fry for a few minutes. Add the left over soup / stock and mix well. Simmer on low heat till almost dry and dark in colour.

14. PORK TROTTERS CURRY

Serves 6   Time required: 1 hour

Ingredients
8 pig Trotters preferably the front ones
2 large tomatoes pureed or chopped finely
3 teaspoons chillie powder
2 large onions chopped
1 teaspoon coriander powder
1 teaspoon all spice powder or garam masala powder
3 tablespoons oil
Salt to taste
3 tablespoons chopped coriander leaves

Wash the trotters well and cook it with sufficient water and a little salt in a pressure cooker till tender.
Heat the oil in a pan and lightly sauté the onions. Add the cooked trotters all the above ingredients and mix well. Cook first on high heat then on low heat for for about 15 minutes till the gravy thickens.. Serve hot with rice or bread or even dosas or hoppers.

15. PORK STEAKS AND POTATOES

Serves 6   Time required: 45 minutes

Ingredients
1 kg pork loin sliced into steaks with a little fat and lard
3 teaspoons roughly ground black pepper
1 teaspoon sugar
1 teaspoon ginger garlic paste
2 tablespoons Worcestershire sauce

1 tablespoon tomato sauce
2 tablespoons vinegar
½ teaspoon turmeric powder
Salt to taste
4 tablespoons oil
3 boiled potatoes peeled and cut into 3 or 4 thick rounds

Boil the pork steaks with a little salt and a pinch of turmeric in some water till just tender. Drain the remaining soup and keep aside.

Place the cooked pork steaks flat on a plate. Mix all the above ingredients together in a small bowl. Coat each steak well on both sides and keep in the fridge for a couple of hours.
Heat the oil in a suitable pan and fry the Steaks, a few at a time, till brown on each side. Pour any remaining marinade into the remaining oil and fry till almost dry. Mix in the boiled potato rounds and remove from heat. Arrange the pork steaks and potatoes in a serving dish.
Serve with steamed or braised vegetables and bread

D. FISH / PRAWNS / CRABS & EGGS
(THESE RECIPES CAN BE ADAPTED
FOR EITHER FRESH WATER OR SEA FISH)

1. MACKEREL OR SARDINE VINDALOO

Serves 6   Time required: 45 minutes

Ingredients
1 kg good fleshy mackerels or sardines each cut into half
2 medium sized onions chopped
2 teaspoons chillie powder
2 teaspoons cumin powder
2 teaspoons ginger garlic paste
2 tablespoons vinegar

Salt to taste
2 tomatoes pureed or chopped finely
2 tablespoons oil

Wash and clean the mackerels or sardines well and lightly fry in a little oil till the pieces become firm.
Heat more oil in the same pan and add the onions and fry till golden brown. Add the ginger garlic paste and sauté for a while. Add the chillie powder, cumin powder, tomato, vinegar and salt and fry for some time. Add 2 cups of water and bring to boil. Drop in the mackerel or sardines and mix well. Cook till the gravy is slightly thick.

(Slices of Shark fish can also be used in this recipe to make Shark Fish Vindaloo. However the pieces need not be fried beforehand since shark meat is quite firm)

2. TANGY SALMON CURRY

Serves 6   Time required: 20 minutes

Ingredients
1 kg Salmon fish cut into slices
2 onions sliced
2 green chillies sliced lengthwise
1 teaspoon chopped garlic
1 teaspoon coriander powder
½ teaspoon turmeric powder
2 teaspoons chillie powder
2 cups tamarind water extracted from a lime sized ball
Salt to taste
2 tablespoons Oil

Heat oil in a suitable vessel and sauté the onions and garlic for about 2 or 3 minutes. Add the green chillies, coriander powder, turmeric powder, chillie powder, salt and tamarind water and bring to boil. Drop in the Salmon slices and mix well. Cover and simmer on low heat for about 8 minutes till the fish is cooked and the gravy is thick

3. SARDINES IN TOMATO GRAVY

Serves 6   Time required: 20 minutes

Ingredients
1 kg Sardines
3 tablespoons oil
2 teaspoons ginger garlic paste
3 tomatoes pureed or chopped finely
1 teaspoon chillie powder
2 teaspoons coriander powder
Salt to taste
¼ teaspoon turmeric powder
3 onions sliced finely

Wash the sardines and keep aside.
Heat the oil in a pan and sauté the onions for a few minutes. Add the ginger garlic paste, chillie powder, turmeric powder, salt and. tomato and mix well. Sauté for a few minutes till the oil separates from the mixture. Add 1 cup of water and bring to boil. Drop in the sardines and mix well. Simmer on low heat for about 6 to 8 minutes till the sardines are cooked. Don't overcook the sardines.
Serve with rice, bread or chapattis.

4. TAMARIND FISH CURRY

Serves 6   Time required: 45 minutes

Ingredients
1 kg good fleshy fish cut into slices such as seer, king fish etc
1 cup thick tamarind juice extracted from a lime size ball of tamarind
2 big onions chopped finely
2 teaspoons ginger garlic paste
3 teaspoons chillie powder
1 teaspoon cumin powder
2 teaspoons coriander powder
½ teaspoon turmeric powder

Salt to taste
3 tablespoons oil

Wash the fish well and fry it lightly to make it firm.
Heat the oil in a shallow vessel and fry the onions till golden brown. Add the ginger garlic paste, chillie powder, cumin powder, coriander powder, turmeric powder and a little water and fry well for some time. Add the salt, tamarind juice and some more water if more gravy is required and bring to boil. Add the fish and cook for about 6 to 7 minutes till the fish is cooked.
Garnish with chopped coriander leaves and slit green chilies
Serve with Steamed rice and a foogath.

5. SEER FISH MOLEY (FISH STEW)

Serves 6   Time required: 45 minutes

Ingredients
1kg Seer Fish /Spanish Blue Mackerel / King Fish or any other good fleshy fish of your choice sliced thickly
3 big onions sliced finely
4 green chilies sliced lengthwise
1 teaspoon chopped ginger
1 teaspoon chopped garlic
1 teaspoon black pepper powder
1 cup thick coconut milk
1 teaspoon turmeric powder
1 teaspoon coriander powder
4 tablespoons oil
Salt to taste
1 tablespoon lime / lemon juice
3 tablespoons oil
1 medium size tomato chopped into 8 pieces
8 to 10 curry leaves

Wash the fish well and rub all over with the turmeric powder and a little salt. Heat oil in a flat pan and lightly fry the fish till the pieces are firm. Keep aside.

In the same pan add a little more oil and sauté the sliced onions, garlic, ginger and curry leaves till the onions turn light brown.

Add the coriander powder and fry for a minute. Add the lime juice, green chillies, salt, coconut milk and 1 cup of water and mix well. Now add the fish. Shake the pan so that the fish is covered with the mixture. Cook on low heat for about 5 or 6 minutes. Now add the tomatoes and pepper powder and turn off the heat. Shake the dish so that the tomatoes and pepper get mixed with the stew. Serve with Hoppers, Bread or steamed rice

Note: The tomatoes should not get cooked. They are added to give some colour to the dish. The pepper added in the end gives it an irresistible aroma.

6. SIMPLE FISH CURRY IN COCONUT MILK

Serves 6   Time required: 45 minutes

Ingredients
1 kg of any good fleshy fish such as Pomfret, Seer, Mullet or Salmon sliced thickly
2 big onions sliced finely
3 green chilies sliced lengthwise
2 teaspoons ginger garlic paste
1cup thick coconut milk
½ teaspoon turmeric powder
3 tablespoons oil
Salt to taste
½ cup tamarind water from a small ball of tamarind
3 teaspoons chillie powder
1 teaspoon cumin powder
1 teaspoon coriander powder
2 sprigs curry leaves

Clean and cut the fish into thick slices.
Heat oil in a pan and add the curry leaves and onions and sauté for a few minutes. Add the ginger garlic paste, turmeric powder, chillie powder, coriander powder, cumin powder, and tamarind water and fry for 2 or

3 minutes. Add the coconut milk, salt and slit green chillies and a little more water if more gravy is required and bring to boil. Add the fish. Cook on low heat for about 7 to 8 minutes till the fish is cooked. Pour a tablespoon of oil on top then remove from heat. Shake the pan so that the oil coats the top evenly.
(Care should be taken not to overcook the fish or else it will break up.)
Serve with rice or bread

7. FISH AND GREEN MANGO CURRY

Serves 6   Time required: 45 minutes

Ingredients
1 kg of any good fleshy fish cut into medium pieces
2 teaspoons ginger garlic paste
3 green chilies
3 tablespoons coriander leaves
1 teaspoon cumin powder
2 teaspoons chillie powder
½ teaspoon turmeric powder
1 teaspoon coriander powder
Salt to taste
3 tablespoons oil
2 green mangoes peeled and chopped into medium size pieces
2 onions sliced finely
½ cup coconut paste

Cook the green mango pieces with the green chillies and a pinch of turmeric in a little water till soft. Keep aside

Heat oil in a pan and fry the onions till golden brown. Add the turmeric powder, chillie powder, ginger garlic paste, cumin powder, coriander powder, coconut paste and salt and mix well. Keep frying on low heat till the oil separates from the mixture. Add the fish and the cooked mango pieces and a little more water if required and cook for 7 to 8 minutes till the fish is done. Garnish with the chopped coriander leaves. Serve hot with steamed rice.

8. HOT AND SOUR SALT / DRY FISH CURRY

Serves 6   Time required: 45 minutes

Ingredients
6 to 8 pieces of good salt / dry fish or Bombay Duck
½ cup thick tamarind juice extracted from a lime size ball of tamarind
2 big onions chopped finely
2 tablespoons ginger garlic paste
3 teaspoons chillie powder
1 teaspoon cumin powder
2 teaspoons coriander powder
½ teaspoon turmeric powder
Salt to taste
3 tablespoons oil
2 tomatoes chopped

Soak the salt fish for about 1 hour in a little water, then rinse the pieces well. Fry the salt fish pieces or Bombay Duck lightly in a little oil to make them firm.
Heat the oil in a shallow vessel and fry the onions till golden brown. Add the ginger garlic paste, chillie powder, cumin powder, coriander powder, turmeric powder, chopped tomatoes and a little water and fry well for some time. Add the salt, tamarind juice and some more water if gravy is required and bring to boil. Add the salt fish and simmer for about 5 minutes for the salt fish to absorb the gravy. Garnish with chopped coriander leaves and slit green chilies.

9. SIMPLE FRIED FISH

Serves 6   Time required: 45 minutes

Ingredients
8 or 10 slices of any good fleshy fish
2 teaspoons chillie powder
1 teaspoon turmeric powder
Salt to taste
Oil for frying

Wash the fish and marinate with the chillie powder, salt, and turmeric powder for about 15 minutes.

Heat the oil in a flat pan and shallow fry the pieces about 4 at a time till nice and brown on both sides. Serve with bread and chips.

This is also a good accompaniment to pepper water and rice. It could also be served as a snack. (For a more crispy fish, coat the fish slices with a little semolina or rice flour)

10. FRIED WHOLE FISH – POMFRET OR MACKEREL

Serves 6   Time required: 45 minutes

Ingredients
6 medium size Pomfrets or Mackerels
3 tablespoons oil
3 teaspoons chillie powder
1 teaspoon pepper powder
2 teaspoons ginger garlic paste
1 teaspoon cumin powder
1teaspoon coriander powder
½ teaspoon turmeric powder
2 teaspoons lime juice or tamarind juice
1teaspoon salt
2 tablespoons coconut paste (optional)

Clean and remove the scales, fins and insides of the fish. Wash well.
Mix all the above ingredients together with a little water to form a paste. Slit each pomfret or mackerel lengthwise on either side keeping the center bone intact. Stuff the paste into each fish very evenly on either side of the center bone. Rub some of the paste on the outsides as well. Heat oil in a flat pan and shallow fry the fish two at a time on both sides till evenly brown. Serve with steamed rice or bread along with onion rings and chips.

Note: The fish could be baked instead of fried if desired. Baste the fish with sufficient oil then bake in a medium oven (180 Degrees) for 25 to 30 minutes or till nicely browned,

11. FISH POTATO CHOPS (FISH POTATO CUTLETS)

Serves 6   Time required: 1 hour

Ingredients
300 grams good fleshy fish fillets
2 teaspoons chopped mint
1 teaspoon ground black pepper / pepper powder
Salt to taste
2 tablespoons tomato sauce
2 green chillies chopped finely
1 teaspoon butter
1 egg beaten
3 tablespoons oil
3 tablespoons bread crumbs
1 cup boiled and mashed potatoes
Wash the fish and cook in a little water with some salt till soft. Remove from the heat and cool. When cold mash the fish with a fork. Mix in the, mint, pepper, salt, chillies, tomato sauce and butter. Divide the mashed potato into equal portions. Form into oval shapes. Make a depression in each and fill with a little of the fish mixture.
Now heat the oil in a flat pan. Dip each Chop / cutlet in the beaten egg, then shallow fry on both sides till brown. Serve as a side dish or a snack.

12. SPICY FISH CUTLETS

Serves 6   Time required: 1 hour

Ingredients
300 grams good fleshy Hilsa or any other fleshy fish cut into fillets
2 teaspoons chopped coriander leaves
1 medium size onion chopped finely
1 teaspoon chopped ginger
1 teaspoon all spice powder or garam masala powder
1 teaspoon cumin powder
1 teaspoon coriander powder
1 teaspoon chillie powder
Salt to taste

3 green chillies chopped finely
1 egg beaten and mixed with 1 tablespoon flour
Oil for frying
1 cup boiled and mashed potatoes

Heat 2 tablespoons oil in a pan and add the onions, green chillies and chopped ginger and fry till golden brown. Add the fish fillets, garam masala powder / all spice powder, cumin powder, coriander powder, chillie powder and salt and mix well. Fry for a few minutes. Add ¼ cup water and cook till the fish is cooked and all the water dries up.
Remove from heat and when cold mash the fish with a fork. Mix in the mashed potato and the coriander leaves. Divide into equal portions. Pat into oval shapes and flatten with a knife. Heat the oil in a flat pan. Dip each Cutlet in the beaten egg, then shallow fry on both sides till brown.

13. TUNA FISH CROQUETTES

Serves 6   Time required: 45 minutes

Ingredients
1 can of Tuna fish
2 teaspoons chopped mint
1 teaspoon ground black pepper / pepper powder
Salt to taste
2 tablespoons tomato sauce
1 teaspoon butter
1 egg beaten
Yolk of one egg
3 tablespoons oil
3 tablespoons bread crumbs
1 cup boiled and mashed potatoes

Drain away the brine from the Tuna then mash the fish with a fork. Mix in the mashed potatoes, mint, pepper, salt, tomato sauce, butter and the egg yolk. Form into croquettes (cigar shape).

Heat the oil in a flat pan. Dip each croquette in the beaten eggs, roll in bread crumbs then shallow fry on all sides till brown. Drain and serve with tartar sauce.

14. BRAISED FISH STEAKS

Serves 6   Time required: 1 hour

Ingredients
1 kg good fleshy fish such as Sea Bass, Bassa, Tilapia, Cod, etc cut into thick boneless wedges or steaks
2 teaspoons ginger garlic paste
2 tablespoons red chillie powder
1 teaspoon ground black pepper / pepper powder
2 tablespoons Worcestershire sauce
1 tablespoon tomato sauce
Salt to taste
6 tablespoons oil
3 tablespoons mixed bread crumbs and crushed cornflakes
1 egg beaten

Mix all the ingredients together (except the oil, egg and bread crumbs and corn flakes) with a little water. Marinate the fish with this paste and keep aside for 1 hour. Dip the Fish steaks in beaten egg then roll in a mixture of powdered corn flakes and bread crumbs. Heat oil in a shallow pan and fry the fish on both sides till brown. Use a little more oil if necessary. Serve with bread and steamed or braised vegetables and white sauce

15. SIMPLE FISH CUTLETS

Serves 6   Time required: 45 minutes

Ingredients
1 kg firm fleshy fish cut into thick wedges
3 onions minced well
2 green chilies minced
2-teaspoons chillie powder

½ teaspoon turmeric powder
1 teaspoon cumin powder
1 teaspoon ginger garlic paste
Salt to taste
Oil for frying

Wash the fish pieces well then boil in a little water with a pinch of turmeric and a little salt till soft. Drain the water. Crumble into mince when slightly cold and mix in all the above ingredients. Form into even sized balls, then flatten each to form small cutlets.

Make a mixture of one beaten egg, 2 tablespoons plain flour, and a pinch of salt.
Heat the oil in a suitable pan. Coat each fish cutlet with the egg and flour mixture and shallow fry a few cutlets at a time till golden brown on both sides. Serve as a snack with tomato sauce or as a side dish

16. FRIED SALT FISH / BOMBAY DUCK

Serves 6   Time required: 45 minutes

Ingredients
8 or 10 pieces of salt fish or dried Bombay Ducks
2 teaspoons chillie powder
1 teaspoon turmeric powder
1 tablespoon vinegar
6 tablespoons oil for frying

Soak the Salt Fish / Bombay Ducks in a bowl of water for about 15 minutes, then wash well so as to remove all the sandy residues. Cut into suitable pieces fi too big. Coat them with the chillie powder, vinegar and turmeric powder. Heat the oil in a flat pan and shallow fry the pieces about 3 at a time, till nice and brown on both sides. Serve with Pepper water and rice.

17. PRAWN JALFREZIE

Serves 6   Time required: 1 hour

Ingredients
500 grams cleaned and de-veined prawns
1 teaspoon cumin seeds
3 dry red chillies broken into bits
2 green chillies slit
1 teaspoon ginger garlic paste
2 tomatoes chopped
2 onions sliced finely
1 capsicum chopped into small pieces
1 teaspoon spice powder or garam masala powder
1 teaspoon pepper powder
3 tablespoons oil
Salt to taste

Heat oil in a suitable pan and add the dry red chillies and cumin seeds.
When they begin to splutter add the onions and fry till golden brown. Add
the prawns and stir fry for a few minutes till they change colour. Now add
all the other ingredients and very little water and stir well. Simmer on low
heat till the prawns are cooked and the gravy has almost dried up. Serve
with rice and Pepper Water or with chapattis, bread, etc.

18. SIMPLE PRAWN / SHRIMP CURRY

Serves 6   Time required: 45 minutes

Ingredients
1 kg medium size Shrimps / Prawns cleaned and de-veined
2 tomatoes pureed
3 onions sliced finely
2 teaspoons chillie powder
½ teaspoon turmeric powder
1 teaspoon cumin powder
1 teaspoon coriander powder
Salt to taste

1 teaspoon ginger garlic paste
3 tablespoons oil
2 tablespoons vinegar

Marinate the shrimps / prawns with the chillie powder, turmeric powder, cumin powder, coriander powder, vinegar and salt and keep aside for 15 minutes.
Heat oil in a pan and fry the onions till golden brown. Add the ginger garlic paste and tomato and fry for a few minutes. Add the marinated prawns / shrimps and mix well. Add 1 cup of water and cook on medium heat for about 10 minutes till the prawns / shrimps are cooked. Garnish with chopped coriander leaves.
Serve with rice, Bread or Chapattis.

19. PRAWN VINDALOO

Serves 6   Time required: 45 minutes

Ingredients
1 kg fresh Shrimps or Prawns shelled and de-veined
2 medium sized onions chopped
2 teaspoons chillie powder
2 teaspoons cumin powder
½ teaspoon pepper powder
2 teaspoons ginger garlic paste
3 tablespoons vinegar
Salt to taste
2 potatoes boiled, peeled and cut into quarters
3 tablespoons oil

Wash and de-vein the prawns well and keep aside. Heat oil in a pan and add the onions and fry till light brown. Add the ginger garlic paste and sauté for a while. Add the chillie powder, cumin powder, pepper powder, Vinegar and salt and fry for some time till the oil separates from the mixture. Now add the prawns and mix well. Add a little more water and cook till the gravy is slightly thick and the prawns are cooked. Mix in the boiled potatoes. Simmer for 2 minutes then remove from heat. Serve with steamed rice or any Indian Bread

20. PRAWN BHOONI FRY / PRAWN AND DILL LEAVES FRY

Serves 6   Time required: 1 hour

Ingredients
½ kg prawns cleaned and de-veined
1 cup fresh dill leaves or fenugreek leaves washed and chopped
½ teaspoon turmeric powder
2 teaspoons chillie powder
1 teaspoon cumin powder
1 teaspoon coriander powder
3 tomatoes chopped
3 onions chopped finely
Salt to taste
3 tablespoons oil
2 teaspoons ginger garlic paste

Wash and de-vein the prawns well.. Heat half the oil in a suitable pan and add the prawns and a pinch of turmeric and stir fry till the prawns are half cooked and the water dries up. Keep aside.

In the same pan add the remaining oil and fry the onions till golden brown. Now add the chopped tomatoes and ginger garlic paste and sauté till the tomatoes are reduced to pulp. Add the dill or fenugreek leaves, chillie powder, turmeric powder, salt, coriander powder and cumin powder and mix well. Cook till the tomatoes turn to pulp and the leaves shrivel up. Add the cooked prawns and stir-fry for a few minutes. Add a little water and simmer for a few more minutes till the gravy is thick.

Note: The same Prawn Curry could be cooked with Dil leaves, Ridge Gourd, Zucchini, Gherkins, etc

21. SPICY PRAWN FRY

Serves 6   Time required: 45 minutes

Ingredients
½ kg medium sized prawns cleaned and de-veined
2 teaspoons chillie powder
1 teaspoon turmeric powder
1 teaspoon cumin powder
1 teaspoon pepper powder
1 teaspoon all spice powder / garam masala powder
2 onions sliced finely
Juice of one lime
Salt to taste
4 tablespoons oil
2 tablespoons chopped coriander leaves for garnishing

Wash the prawns well and mix in the chillie powder, turmeric powder, cumin powder, pepper powder, all spice / garam masala powder, lime juice and salt.

Heat the oil in a large pan and sauté the onions for some time. Add the marinated prawns and mix well. Cook on low heat till the prawns are cooked. Keep frying till all the water dries up. Garnish with chopped coriander leaves.
Serve as a side dish or as a snack or starter

22. PRAWN FRITTERS

Serves 6   Time required: 45 minutes

Ingredients
300 grams cleaned and de-veined prawns
1 teaspoon ground black pepper / pepper powder
Salt to taste
6 tablespoons flour or maida
1 teaspoon cornflour
Oil for deep frying

Boil the prawns with a pinch of turmeric, ½ teaspoon chillie powder and a pinch of salt in a little water till half cooked. Drain away the water.

Make a batter with the flour, salt, pepper, corn flour and ½ cup of water. Mix the prawns in the batter. Heat the oil in a suitable frying pan. Drop in the coated prawns one at a time in the hot oil, (as many as the pan can hold) and fry till brown and crisp. (Add a little more flour if the batter is too thin). Serve hot with tomato sauce.

23. PRAWN AND POTATO CUTLETS

Serves 6   Time required: 1 hour

Ingredients
300 grams cleaned and de-veined Prawns
3 potatoes boiled and mashed
2 teaspoons chopped mint
1 teaspoon pepper powder
Salt to taste
1 egg beaten
3 tablespoons oil
3 tablespoons bread crumbs

Wash the prawns well and cook in a little water with some salt and a pinch of pepper and turmeric till tender. Remove and keep aside to cool.
When cold, mix in the mashed potatoes, mint, pepper and salt. Form into oval shapes and flatten with a knife.
Heat the oil in a flat pan. Dip each cutlet in the beaten egg, roll in bread crumbs, then shallow fry on both sides till brown. Drain and serve hot with Tomato sauce / ketchup.

24. SPICY CRAB CURRY

Serves 6   Time required: 45 minutes

Ingredients
6 to 8 medium sized crabs or 5 big ones cleaned and shelled
2 big onions sliced finely
2 teaspoons coriander powder
2 teaspoons chillie powder
2 teaspoons ginger and garlic paste
Salt to taste
2 or 3 tablespoons oil
½ teaspoon turmeric powder
1 teaspoon cumin powder
2 tablespoons chopped coriander leaves

Clean and wash the crabs well and keep aside.
Heat oil in a pan and sauté the onions and ginger garlic paste for some time. Add the chillie powder, coriander powder, turmeric powder, salt and a little water and fry till the oil separates from the mixture. Now add the crabs and mix well. Add a little water. Cover and cook on low heat for about 10 minutes till the gravy is very thick. Serve with bread or rice

25. GREEN MASALA CRAB CURRY

Serves 6   Time required: 45 minutes

Ingredients
6 or 7 medium size crabs
2 onions chopped
2 tomatoes chopped
1 teaspoon chillie powder
1 teaspoon coriander powder
1 cup chopped coriander leaves
4 tablespoons grated coconut
4 green chillies
3 cloves
2 one inch pieces of cinnamon
1 teaspoon ginger garlic paste

Salt to taste
2 teaspoons oil

Clean and wash the crabs well.
Grind the coriander leaves, coconut, cloves, cinnamon and green chillies together to a smooth paste.

Heat the oil in a suitable pan and sauté the onions till light brown. Add the ginger garlic paste and sauté for a few minutes. Add the chopped tomatoes, chillie powder, coriander powder, cumin powder, salt and continue frying till the oil separates from the mixture and the tomatoes are reduced to pulp. Mix in the ground green paste and stir fry for a few minutes. Add 2 cups of water and bring to boil. Add the crabs and simmer for about 10 minutes till the crabs are cooked and the gravy is thick. Remove from heat. Garnish with chopped coriander leaves. Serve with rice or bread.

26. SIMPLE EGG CURRY

Serves 6   Time required: 45 minutes

Ingredients
6 eggs
2 onions chopped
2 tomatoes chopped
2 teaspoons chillie powder
1 teaspoon coriander powder
2 tablespoons chopped coriander leaves
1 teaspoon ginger garlic paste
Salt to taste
2 teaspoons oil

Boil and eggs and shell them. Cut each hardboiled egg in half lengthwise. Heat the oil in a suitable pan and sauté the onions till golden brown. Add the ginger garlic paste and fry for a few minutes. Add the chopped tomatoes, chillie powder, coriander powder and salt, and continue frying till the oil separates from the mixture and the tomatoes are reduced to pulp. Add about ½ cup of water and bring to boil. When the gravy is thick add the halved hard-boiled eggs and simmer for a few minutes. Garnish with chopped coriander leaves. Serve with rice or bread.

27. EGG VINDALOO

Serves 6   Time required: 45 minutes

Ingredients
6 Hard boiled eggs shelled
2 onions chopped
2 teaspoons chillie powder
½ teaspoon turmeric powder
2 teaspoons ginger garlic paste
1 teaspoon cumin powder
½ cup tomato puree or tomato paste
2 pieces cinnamon
2 table spoons vinegar
1 teaspoon sugar
Salt to taste
3 tablespoons oil

Heat the oil in a pan and sauté the onions till golden brown. Add the ginger garlic paste and cinnamon fry for some time. Add the chillie powder, cumin powder, turmeric powder, sugar and tomato puree and fry till the oil separates from the mixture. Now add the vinegar and a little water and bring to boil. Reduce heat and simmer till the gravy is sufficiently thick. Cut the boiled eggs into halves and carefully drop into the gravy. Simmer for a few minutes. Take out the egg halves and place on a serving dish. Pour the thick gravy over the eggs and shake the dish so that all the eggs are covered with the gravy. Serve hot with white steamed rice or coconut rice or bread.

28. EGG AND BRINJAL (AUBERGINE) CURRY

Serves 6   Time required: 45 minutes

Ingredients
6 hard boiled eggs, peeled and halved
500 grams round or long Brinjals (Aubergines) cut into big pieces
2 tablespoons vinegar
Salt to taste
2 onions chopped finely
1 teaspoon finely chopped garlic
1 teaspoon finely chopped ginger
2 tablespoons Oil
¼ teaspoon turmeric powder
1 teaspoon cumin powder
2 teaspoon chillie powder
1 small piece of cinnamon
3 cloves
2 tablespoons tomato paste or juice
2 tablespoons chopped coriander leaves

Fry the onions, cloves, cinamon, and c hopped garlic and ginger gently in the oil until golden brown. Add the chillie powder, turmeric powder, cumin powder and fry for a few minutes. Add the Brinjals / Aubergines, vinegar, salt and the tomato paste / juice and one cup of water. Cook on low heat for about 8 to 10 minutes or till the brinjals are cooked but firm. Now drop in the hard boiled eggs. Mix carefully. Garnish with chopped fresh coriander leaves. Serve with bread, rice or chapattis.

29. EGG DROP CURRY OR POACHED EGGS CURRY

Egg Curries are usually made with boiled eggs. In this recipe, the raw egg is poured into hot gravy then poached in the gravy till the eggs are cooked. One of the earliest innovations in Anglo-Indian Cooking.

Serves 6   Time required: 45 minutes

Ingredients
6 Eggs

2 large tomatoes chopped
2 tablespoons cooking oil
1 large onion sliced finely
2 green chillies chopped fine
1 teaspoon minced garlic
2 teaspoons chillie powder
1 teaspoon cumin powder
1 teaspoon coriander powder
1 tablespoon vinegar
Salt to taste

Heat the oil in a pan and add the chopped onion, green chillis and garlic and fry till the onions turn light brown. Add the tomatoes, chillie powder, cumin powder, coriander powder, salt, and vinegar and fry for some time. Add ½ cup of water and simmer on low heat till the gravy thickens. Press the back of a large spoon or ladle in the thick gravy to make 6 depressions. Break an egg in each of the depressions. Cover the pan with a lid. Simmer for 4 or 5 more minutes till the eggs are cooked then turn off the heat. Sprinkle a little salt and pepper on the eggs. Serve each egg with a little gravy on to 6 plates taking care not to break the eggs. Serve hot with rice or chapattis

30. BOILED EGGS AND GREEN MANGO CURRY

Serves 6   Time required: 45 minutes

Ingredients
6 or 8 hard boiled eggs, shelled and halved
1 teaspoon ginger garlic paste
3 green chilies
3 tablespoons coriander leaves
1 teaspoon cumin powder
2 teaspoons chillie powder
½ teaspoon turmeric powder
Salt to taste
3 tablespoons oil
2 green mangoes peeled and chopped into medium size pieces
2 onions sliced finely

Cook the green mango pieces with the green chillies and a pinch of turmeric in a little water till soft.

Heat oil in a pan and fry the onions till golden brown. Add the turmeric powder, chillie powder, ginger garlic paste, cumin powder, and salt and mix well. Keep frying on low heat till the oil separates from the mixture. Add the boiled eggs and the cooked mango pieces and a little more water if required and simmer for about 5 more minutes. Garnish with the chopped coriander leaves. Serve hot with steamed rice or chapattis.

31. EGG MOILEE

Serves 6   Time required: 45 minutes

Ingredients
6 hard boiled eggs shelled and halved
2 big onions sliced finely
8 to 10 green chilies sliced lengthwise
1 teaspoon chopped ginger
1 teaspoon chopped garlic
1cup thick coconut milk
½ teaspoon turmeric powder
3 tablespoons oil
Salt to taste

Heat oil in a suitable pan and lightly fry the boiled egg for about 3 minutes. When they turn light brown add all the other ingredients. Mix lightly so that all the Egg halves get covered. Cook on medium heat till the gravy thickens. Serve with rice or bread.

32. EGG POTATO CHOPS

Serves 6   Time required: 40 minutes

Ingredients
6 hard-boiled eggs
3 potatoes boiled and mashed

2 slices bread
3 teaspoons chopped coriander leaves
2 green chillies chopped
½ teaspoon ground black pepper / pepper powder
3 tablespoons bread crumbs
½ teaspoon chopped ginger
Salt to taste
1 egg beaten

Cut the Hardboiled eggs into halves. Soak the bread in water, squeeze and crush. Mix with the mashed potato and all the other ingredients *(except the bread crumbs and beaten eggs).*
Make even sized balls of the mashed potato and place the hardboiled egg halves in the centre. Cover the eggs well with the potato mixture and flatten to form oval shaped cutlets. Dip each cutlet in the beaten egg then roll in bread crumbs and shallow fry in hot oil on both sides till golden brown. Serve hot with mint chutney or tomato ketch up

----

E. VEGETABLE CURRIES AND SIDE DISHES

1. MIXED VEGETABLE VINDALOO

Serves 6   Time required: 45 minutes

Ingredients
½ kg of chopped mixed vegetables such as peas, carrots, potato, cauliflower etc,
2 onions chopped
2 teaspoons chillie powder,
½ teaspoon turmeric powder
2 teaspoons ginger garlic paste,
1 teaspoon cumin powder
2 tomatoes chopped
1 small piece cinnamon
2 tablespoons vinegar

1 teaspoon sugar
Salt to taste,
3 tablespoons oil

Heat the oil in a pan and sauté the onions till golden brown. Add the ginger garlic paste, tomatoes, and cinnamon and fry for some time. Now add the chillie powder, cumin powder, turmeric powder, vinegar and sugar and fry till the oil separates from the mixture. Add the chopped vegetables, and a little water and bring to boil. Reduce heat and simmer till the vegetables are cooked and the gravy is sufficiently thick. Serve with rice or with Puris or any Indian Bread.

2. SIMPLE POTATO CURRY

Serves 6   Time required: 30 minutes

Ingredients
3 potatoes peeled and cut into medium size pieces
2 teaspoons chillie powder
1 teaspoon cumin powder,
1 teaspoon garlic and ginger paste
1 teaspoon coriander powder,
½ teaspoon turmeric powder
2 onions sliced
2 tablespoons oil,
Salt to taste
2 cloves,
1 piece cinnamon

Heat oil in a pan and sauté the onions, cloves and cinnamon for a few minutes. Add all the other ingredients and 2 cups of water and mix well. Cook on low heat till the potatoes are cooked. Serve hot with plain rice/ puris/ chapattis / rotis.

3. POTATO, PEAS AND CAULIFLOWER CURRY

Serves 6   Time required: 45 minutes

Ingredients
1 medium size cauliflower cut into florets
2 potatoes peeled and cut into medium size pieces
½ cup green peas either fresh or frozen
1 tomato chopped,
3 tablespoons ground coconut
2 teaspoons chillie powder
½ teaspoon turmeric
½ teaspoon cumin powder
Salt to taste
1 teaspoon coriander powder
2 small pieces cinamon
1 bay leaf
2 tablespoons oil
1onion chopped
1 tablespoon chopped coriander leaves

Heat the oil in a pan and sauté the onions, cinnamon and bay leaf for a little while. Add the tomatoes, chillie powder, turmeric, coriander powder, spice powder / garam masala powder, cumin powder and salt and stir fry for a few minutes till the tomatoes turn pulpy. Add the cauliflower, potatoes and the ground coconut and mix well. Add 2 cups of water and simmer on low heat till the potatoes are cooked the gravy thickens. Garnish with chopped coriander leaves. Serve with rice or Chapattis.

4. BRINJAL AND POTATO VINDALOO

Serves 6   Time required: 45 minutes

Ingredients
½ kg medium sized round brinjals / eggplant
2 potatoes boiled and peeled
2 onions chopped
2 teaspoons chillie powder

½ teaspoon turmeric powder
2 teaspoons ginger garlic paste
1 teaspoon cumin powder
½ cup tomato puree
2 pieces cinnamon
2 table spoons vinegar
1teaspoon sugar
Salt to taste
3 tablespoons oil

Cut the brinjals / eggplants into halves and wash well.
Heat the oil in a pan and sauté the onions till golden brown. Add the ginger garlic paste and cinnamon and fry for some time. Now add the chillie powder, cumin powder, turmeric powder, sugar and tomato puree and fry till the oil separates from the mixture. Now add the cut brinjals, vinegar and a little water and bring to boil. Reduce heat and simmer till the gravy is sufficiently thick. Mix in the boiled potatoes. Serve with rice or any Indian bread

5. LADY'S FINGERS / OKRA CURRY

Serves 6   Time required: 45 minutes

Ingredients
½ kg tender lady's finger / okra
1 cup tamarind juice extracted from a lime size ball of tamarind
2 teaspoons chillie powder
1 teaspoon turmeric powder
1 teaspoon ginger and garlic paste
A few curry leaves
Salt to taste
2 tablespoons oil,
1 teaspoon cumin powder
2 tablespoons sugar
2 onions chopped

Wash the lady's finger and cut them into medium size pieces. Heat oil in pan and fry the onions till light brown. Add the ginger and garlic paste and sauté for a few minutes. Add the chillie powder, cumin powder, curry leaves, turmeric powder and cumin powder and fry for some time. Add the cut lady's finger and mix well. Keep frying for a few minutes. Now add the salt, sugar and tamarind juice and simmer on low heat till the lady's finger / okra is cooked and the gravy is thick. Serve as a side dish with rice or chapattis

6. SNAKE GOURD / SERPENT GOURD IN COCONUT GRAVY

Serves 6   Time required: 1 hour

Ingredients
1 medium size snake gourd cut into medium size pieces
3 tablespoons ground coconut / coconut paste
2 teaspoons chillie powder,
½ teaspoon turmeric powder
½ teaspoon cumin powder
Salt to taste
1 teaspoon coriander powder
2 tablespoons oil
1 onion chopped
1 tomato chopped
1 tablespoon chopped coriander leaves

Heat the oil in a pan and sauté the onions for a little while. Add the tomatoes, chillie powder, turmeric, coriander powder, cumin powder and salt and stir fry for a few minutes till the tomatoes turn pulpy. Add the snake gourd and the ground coconut and mix well. Add 2 cups of water and simmer on low heat till the snake gourd is cooked and the gravy thickens. Garnish with chopped coriander leaves. Serve with rice or Chapattis.

7. DRUMSTICK AND POTATO CURRY

Serves 6   Time required: 30 minutes

Ingredients
6 drumsticks, peeled and cut into 2 inch pieces
3 potatoes peeled and cut in chunks

2 onions finely chopped,
1 teaspoon ginger garlic paste
2 tomatoes finely chopped
2 tablespoons coriander leaves finely chopped
2 teaspoons chillie powder
1 teaspoon coriander powder
1 teaspoon cumin powder,
½ teaspoon turmeric powder
1 teaspoon garam masala powder / all spice powder
2 green chillies chopped
Salt to taste
2 tablespoons oil

Heat the oil in a pan and sauté the onion for a little while. Add the tomatoes, ginger garlic paste, green chillies, chillie powder, coriander powder, turmeric, garam masala / all spice powder, cumin powder, and salt and stir fry till the oil separates from the mixture. Add the drumsticks and potatoes and 2 cups of water and simmer on low heat till the drum sticks and potatoes are cooked and the gravy thickens. Garnish with chopped coriander leaves.

8. SPINACH AND POTATO FRY

Serves 6   Time required: 45 minutes

Ingredients
3 medium size potatoes peeled and cut into small size pieces
1 cup chopped spinach
2 green chillies chopped finely
6 or 8 curry leaves
½ teaspoon cumin seeds
1 teaspoon chillie powder
Salt to taste
½ teaspoon turmeric powder
2 tablespoons oil

Heat oil in a pan and sauté the cumin seeds, green chillies and curry leaves for a few seconds. Add the potatoes, spinach, chillie powder, turmeric powder and salt and mix well. Add ½ cup of water and mix well. Cover and cook on low heat till the potatoes are cooked and the water dries up. Serve as a side dish.

9. SIMPLE VEGETABLE STEW

Serves 6   Time required: 30 minutes

Ingredients
2 cups of chopped mixed vegetables such as carrot, potato, cauliflower, knoll kol etc
3 onions chopped
3 green chillies slit lengthwise
1 teaspoon chopped garlic
1 teaspoon chopped ginger,
1 teaspoon whole pepper corns
2 cloves
2 pieces cinnamon
1cup thick coconut milk
Salt to taste
2 tablespoons oil.

Heat the oil in a pan and fry the onions till golden brown. Add the green chillies, ginger, garlic, pepper and spices and sauté for a few minutes. Add the vegetables, salt and sufficient water and cook till vegetables are tender. Stir in the coconut milk and simmer for a few minutes. Serve hot with Hoppers or bread.

10. CARROT VICHY (GLAZED CARROTS)

Serves 6 Preparation time 45 minutes

Ingredients
½ kg carrots
2 tablespoons butter
½ teaspoon sugar
1 teaspoon chillie powder

3 green chillies slit lengthwise
1 teaspoon lime juice
1 tablespoon chopped coriander leaves,
Salt to taste

Peel the carrots and cut them into rounds. Boil in sufficient water with one tablespoon vinegar till tender.
Heat the butter in a pan and add the green chillies, boiled carrots, sugar, chillie powder, salt and lime juice. Fry for a couple of minutes then turn off the heat. Garnish with coriander leaves.
Serve as a side dish with steamed rice

11. VEGETABLE JALFRAZIE

Serves 6   Time required: 1 hour

Ingredients
2 medium onions chopped
1 big capsicum / green pepper cut into medium size pieces
½ cup peas
½ cup beans cut finely
2 tomatoes chopped
1 cup cauliflower florets
1 teaspoon coriander powder
2 teaspoons chillie powder
1 teaspoon chopped ginger
1 teaspoon chopped garlic
2 tablespoons vinegar,
2 tablespoons oil
Salt to taste

Heat oil in a suitable pan and sauté the onions, ginger and garlic till golden brown. Add all the other ingredients and stir well. Cook covered on medium heat till the vegetables are cooked. Fry till almost dry. Sir in a teaspoon of butter and serve with rice and pepper water or any bread

12. RADISH AND RED LENTIL (MASOOR DHAL) CURRY

Serves 6   Time required:1 hour

Ingredients
1 cup Red Lentils or Masoor Dhal
4 long white radish peeled and cut into 2 inch piece
2 teaspoons chillie powder
1 teaspoon coriander powder
½ teaspoon turmeric powder
1 teaspoon cumin powder
2 tomatoes chopped
1 teaspoon crushed garlic (optional)
Salt to taste

For the seasoning: 1 teaspoon mustard, 2 red chilies broken into bits and a few curry leaves and 1 tablespoon oil.

Wash the Red Lentils / masoor dhal and cook it along with the tomato, chillie powder, coriander powder, cumin powder, turmeric powder, garlic and radish with sufficient water in a pressure cooker. When done open the cooker, add salt and some more water and mix well.

In another vessel, heat oil and add the mustard, broken red chilies and crushed garlic and fry for some time. When the mustard starts spluttering, pour in the cooked dhal and mix well. Serve with rice

13. VEGETARIAN CHOPS (PATTIES)

Serves 6   Time required: 30 minutes

Ingredients
3 large potatoes boiled and mashed
2 medium size carrots cut into small pieces
10 beans cut into tiny bits
1 medium size onion chopped
1 teaspoon chopped ginger
1 teaspoon chopped garlic

3 green chillies chopped finely
1 teaspoon chopped mint
3 slices bread,
Salt to taste
4 tablespoons oil
2 tablespoons breadcrumbs

Heat 2 tablespoons oil in a pan and fry the onions till golden brown. Add the chopped ginger, garlic and green chillies. Add the carrots and beans and fry well. Sprinkle a little water and simmer till the vegetables are tender and all the water is absorbed. Add the mint and salt and stir well. Remove from heat and cool.
Soak the slices of bread in water for 2 minutes, squeeze dry, mash well and add to the cooked vegetable mixture. Mix in the mashed potato. Form into sausage like shapes and coat with bread crumbs.

Heat the remaining oil in a flat pan and shallow fry the chops till golden brown all over. Serve with tomato sauce or mint chutney.

14. POTATO, BEET & CARROT CHOPS

Serves 6   Time required: 45 minutes

Ingredients
4 potatoes boiled and cut into tiny pieces
1 small beetroot boiled and cut into small pieces
2 medium size carrots boiled and cut into small pieces
1 teaspoon chopped mint
2 green chillies chopped finely
1 teaspoon chopped ginger
1 teaspoon ground black pepper / black pepper powder
1 teaspoon cumin powder
Salt to taste
4 tablespoons oil,
4 tablespoons bread crumbs
2 tablespoons flour (maida)
2 or 3 slices of bread

Mash the potatoes, beet and carrot roughly together and then mix in the salt, chopped mint, chopped green chillies, ginger, pepper powder, cumin powder and flour.

Soak the bread in water for a minute, squeeze dry and mix with the cooked mixture. Form into oval shapes and flatten with a knife.

Heat the oil in a flat pan. Mix the flour with a little water to make a slightly thin paste. Dip each Potato Chop in the flour paste, roll in breadcrumbs then shallow fry on both sides till brown. Drain and serve as a side dish with mint sauce or tomato sauce.

15. POTATO CROQUETTES / RISSOLES

Serves 6   Time required: 30 minutes

Ingredients
½ Kg potatoes boiled and mashed
2 slices bread
3 teaspoons chopped coriander leaves
2 green chillies chopped
½ teaspoon ground black pepper / pepper powder
3 tablespoons bread crumbs
½ teaspoon chopped ginger
Salt to taste
3 tablespoons flour / maida

Soak the bread in water, squeeze and crush. Mix with the mashed potato and all the other ingredients (except the bread crumbs).

Make small balls of the potato dough. Roll and shape into long cigar shaped patties. Mix the flour in a little water to make a paste. Dip each croquette in the flour paste, roll in bread crumbs and shallow fry in hot oil on both sides till golden brown.

Serve hot with mint chutney or tomato ketch up.

16. RAILWAY VEGETABLE CUTLETS

Serves 6   Time required: 45 minutes

Ingredients
1 cup of chopped boiled vegetables such as peas, carrots, French beans etc
3 potatoes boiled and mashed
2 onions chopped finely
2 green chillies chopped
1 teaspoon chopped mint
1 teaspoon finely chopped ginger
1 teaspoon chillie powder
½ teaspoon cumin powder
½ teaspoon coriander powder
Salt to taste
4 tablespoons oil
1 egg beaten
3 tablespoons breadcrumbs

Heat oil in a pan and fry the onions and ginger till golden brown. Add the chopped green chillies and sauté for a few minutes. Now add the cooked vegetables, salt and all the other ingredients and mix well. Cook on low heat for about 5 minutes till all the water dries up. Set aside to cool for some time.
When the mixture is slightly cold, mix in the mashed potato. Make even sized balls with the mixture and form into round cutlets.
Heat the oil in a flat pan. Dip each cutlet in beaten egg, roll in powdered breadcrumbs and shallow fry till golden brown on both sides. Serve hot with tomato sauce or chutney.

17. SIMPLE POTATO CUTLETS

Serves 6   Time required: 30 minutes

Ingredients
4 large potatoes boiled and mashed
2 slices bread
3 teaspoons chopped coriander leaves

2 green chillies chopped
½ teaspoon ground black pepper / pepper powder
½ teaspoon chillie powder
½ teaspoon cumin powder
3 tablespoons bread crumbs
½ teaspoon chopped ginger
Salt to taste
1 egg beaten

Soak the bread in water, squeeze and crush. Mix with the mashed potato and all the other ingredients (except the bread crumbs and beaten eggs). Make small balls of the potato dough. Flatten and shape into patties. Dip each in the beaten Egg, roll in bread crumbs and shallow fry in hot oil on both sides till golden brown. Serve hot with mint chutney or tomato ketch up.

18. DOL (DHAL) AND GREENS CURRY

Serves 6   Time required: 1 hour

Ingredients
1 cup Tur Dhal or Masoor Dal
1 cup of greens chopped finely...spinach or any other greens
2 green chilies slit lengthwise
2 teaspoons chillie powder
1 teaspoon coriander powder
½ teaspoon turmeric powder
2 tomatoes chopped
1 onion chopped.
Salt to taste

To Temper: 1 teaspoon mustard, 2 red chilies broken into bits, 2 pods of garlic smashed, and 1 tablespoon oil.

Wash the dal and cook it along with the greens, tomato, chillie powder, coriander powder, turmeric powder and onion with sufficient water in a pressure cooker. When done, open the cooker, add salt and some more water and mash well.

In another vessel, heat oil and add the mustard, broken red chilies and smashed garlic and fry for some time. When the mustard starts to splutter pour in the cooked dhal. Add a little water if the dal is too thick. Simmer for 2 minutes then remove from heat. Serve with rice.

19. ANGLO-INDIAN DOL MASH (MASHED DHAL)

Serves 6   Time required: 45 minutes

Ingredients
1 cup Tur Dhal or Masoor Dhal
2 onions chopped
2 green chilies chopped
1 teaspoon garlic chopped
1 teaspoon ginger chopped
¼ teaspoon turmeric
¼ teaspoon mustard
A few curry leaves
Salt to taste
1 tablespoon oil

Cook the dhal with sufficient water and ¼ teaspoon turmeric till soft in a pressure cooker. Mash and add salt to it. Keep aside. (The dhal should be thick).
Heat oil in a pan and add the mustard. When it splutters add the chopped onion, green chilies, curry leaves, ginger and garlic and fry well till the onions turn golden brown. Add the cooked and mashed dhal and mix well. Add a little ghee while serving.

20. CABBAGE FOOGATH (CABBAGE FRY)

Serves 6   Time required: 30 minutes

Ingredients
1 fresh medium sized cabbage chopped finely
3 green chilies chopped
1 onion chopped

1 teaspoon chopped garlic
¼ teaspoon mustard seeds
1 sprig curry leaves
½ cup grated coconut (optional)
1 tablespoon oil
Salt to taste

Heat oil in a pan and add the mustard, garlic and curry leaves. When the mustard splutters, add the chopped onion and green chilies and fry till the onions turn slightly brown. Add the Cabbage and salt and mix well. Cover and cook for about 6 to 7 minutes till the cabbage is soft. Add the grated coconut and mix well.

21. GREENS FOOGATH

Serves 6   Time required: 30 minutes

Ingredients
4 bunches of fresh greens of your choice such as spinach, Dill, Amaranth, Drumstick leaves, etc
1 large onion chopped
3 green chilies chopped
Salt to taste
1 tablespoon oil
1 sprig curry leaves.
2 tablespoons grated coconut
½ teaspoon mustard seeds

Chop the greens into fine pieces then wash well and drain. Heat oil in a pan and add the mustard seeds. When they begin to splutter add the onions, green chillies and curry leaves and fry till the onions are slightly brown. Toss in the greens. Add salt and coconut. Cover and cook for a few minutes till all the water dries up and the greens are cooked, then take down.

22. BEANS AND CARROT FOOGATH

Serves 6   Time required: 30 minutes

Ingredients
½ kg string beans chopped finely
3 tender carrots chopped into small pieces
½ cup grated coconut
3 red chilies broken into bits
¼ teaspoon mustard seeds
A few curry leaves

Boil the chopped beans and carrots for about 5 minutes with some water. Strain and keep aside. Heat oil in a pan and add the mustard seeds. When they splutter add the red chilies and curry leaves and fry for a few seconds. Now toss in the boiled beans. Add salt and coconut and mix well. Stir-fry for a few minutes and then take down.

23. CAULIFLOWER FOOGATH

Serves 6   Time required: 45 minutes

Ingredients
1 small cauliflower chopped into small florets
2 or 3 dry red chilies broken into bits
1 onion sliced
2 pods of garlic chopped
¼ teaspoon mustard seeds
1 sprig curry leaves
½ cup grated coconut (optional)
2 tablespoons oil
Salt to taste

Heat oil in a pan and add the mustard, garlic and curry leaves. When the mustard splutters, add the chopped onion and red chilies and fry till the onions turn slightly brown. Add the Cauliflower and salt and mix well. Add ½ cup of water. Cover and cook for about 6 to 7 minutes till the cauliflower is cooked and the water dries up. (Add the grated coconut and mix well) Serve as a side dish with rice and curry.

24. FRIED LADY FINGERS / OKRA

Serves 6   Time required: 30 minutes

Ingredients
½ kg tender lady's finger
1 teaspoons chillie powder
½ teaspoon turmeric powder
Salt to taste
2 tablespoons oil
1 teaspoon cumin powder

Wash the whole lady's fingers and dry them well. Cut into rings discarding the ends. Mix with the chillie powder, cumin powder, turmeric powder, and salt. Heat oil in a pan and fry the lady's fingers till golden brown and crisp.

25. FRIED BITTER GOURD (BITTER MELON FRY)

Serves 6   Time required: 30 minutes

Ingredients
½ kg tender bitter gourd
2 teaspoons chillie powder
½ teaspoon turmeric powder
Salt to taste
2 tablespoons oil
1teaspoon cumin powder

Scrape and wash the bitter gourds then cut them into thin slices. Soak the slices in salt water for about 2 hours to remove the bitterness. Drain and squeeze out the excess water. Mix the bitter gourd slices with the chillie powder, cumin powder, turmeric powder, and salt. Heat the oil in a pan and fry the bitter gourd slices on medium heat till golden brown and crisp.

26. EASY POTATO FRY

Serves 6   Time required: 40 minutes

Ingredients
4 medium size potatoes
3 green chilies chopped into pieces
2 onions chopped finely
1 teaspoon mustard seeds
½ teaspoon chopped ginger
1 tablespoon chopped coriander leaves
½ teaspoon turmeric powder
A few curry leaves
Salt to taste

Wash the potatoes well and boil them till soft. Peel the skins and cut or mash into small pieces. Heat oil in a pan and add the mustard and curry leaves. When the mustard starts spluttering, add the onions and ginger and sauté till the onions are golden brown. Add the turmeric powder and the green chilies and fry for a few minutes. Now add the cooked potatoes and mix well. Remove from heat and serve with Pepper Water and Rice or Dhal and Rice or even chapattis or Rice Pancakes

27. FRIED GHERKINS (IVY GOURD / GENTLEMAN'S TOES)

Serves 6 Preparation Time 45 minutes

Ingredients
½ kg tender gherkins
2 teaspoons chillie powder
1 teaspoon salt
1 teaspoon cumin powder
½ teaspoon turmeric powder
2 tablespoons oil

Wash the gherkins and cut them into thin slices. Mix the gherkin slices with the salt, chillie powder, turmeric powder and cumin powder. Heat oil in a pan and fry the gherkins till brown and crisp. Serve with rice as a side dish.

28. BUTTER FRIED CAULIFLOWER

Serves 6   Time required: 20 minutes

Ingredients
1 big cauliflower cut into medium size florets
2 teaspoons chopped garlic
2 bay leaves
8 pepper corns
1 piece cinnamon (one inch length)
1 teaspoon ground black pepper / pepper powder
2 tablespoons butter
Salt to taste

Wash and soak the cauliflower for 1 hour in warm salt water. Cook the cauliflower in a little water for 5 minutes, then drain.
Heat the butter in a pan and add the bay leaves, pepper corns, cinnamon and garlic and fry for a couple of minutes. Add the cooked cauliflower, salt and pepper and mix well. Fry on low heat for a few seconds then turn off the heat. Garnish with chopped mint or parsley

29. GREEN BANANA CRISPY FRY

Serves 6   Time required: 45 minutes

Ingredients
2 green bananas / plantains
2 teaspoons chillie powder
½ teaspoon turmeric powder
½ teaspoon cumin powder
Salt to taste
Oil for frying

Peel and cut the green bananas into thin slices. Soak in salt water for about 10 minutes. Drain away the water and mix the banana slices with the chillie powder, cumin powder, turmeric powder and salt. Heat oil in a deep pan till smoky. Deep fry a few of the banana slices at a time till golden brown. Serve as a side dish with rice and any curry or as a snack.

30. VEGETABLE MARROW SAUTEED IN BUTTER

Serves 6   Time required: 45 minutes

Ingredients
3 vegetable marrows / chowchow peeled and cut into small pieces,
3 tablespoons butter
Salt and pepper to taste

Heat the butter in a suitable pan. Add the vegetable marrow / chowchow, salt and pepper and mix well. Cover and cook on low heat till the chowchow is cooked and the pieces are not too soft. Take should be taken not to overcook the vegetable.

V

RICE DISHES AND PILAFS

Rice forms an integral part of an Anglo-Indian Lunch Menu. While every day lunch would be steamed white rice with an accompanying meat curry or pepper water and fry and a vegetable foogath or side dish, weekends and festive occasions would see a variety of special spiced rice dishes such as the popular Anglo-Indian Saffron Coconut Rice, Meat Palaus, Biryani, etc

This section covers a few popular Anglo-Indian Rice delicacies

1. PLAIN WHITE STEAMED RICE

Serves 6   Time required: 45 minutes

Ingredients
1 cup raw rice
2 cups water
A pinch of salt

Wash the rice and soak in 2 cups of water and a pinch of salt for 15 minutes. Place on heat and bring to boil. Reduce heat and cook on low heat till done and all the water is absorbed. Cover and allow to stand for 15 minutes before serving. This is the standard plain steamed rice eaten every day. Serve with any curry, dhal or pepper water.

2. SAFFRON COCONUT RICE / YELLOW RICE

Serves 6   Time required: 45 minutes

Ingredients
1 fresh coconut grated and milk extracted to get 4 cups of diluted milk *or*
(1 pack of coconut milk (250 ml) diluted with water to get 4 cups of milk
2 cups of Raw Rice or Basmati Rice
½ teaspoon turmeric powder or a few strands of saffron
Salt to taste
4 tablespoons butter or ghee
3 cloves, 3 cardamoms, 3 small sticks of cinnamon

Heat the ghee in a large vessel or Rice cooker and fry the spices for a few minutes. Add the washed rice, salt, turmeric / saffron and 4 cups of coconut milk and cook till the rice is done.

Coconut Rice is best eaten with Ball Curry or Chicken curry and Devil Chutney.

3. PISH-PASH RICE OR SMASHED RICE

Pish-Pash is a watery Rice and Meat Dish that was very popular in Anglo-Indian homes in the olden days. It was prepared using small bits of meat and rice. The word 'Pash' is of Old English origin, meaning to 'smash' or 'mash' in relation to mashed meat. The term 'Pish Pash' dates back to 18th Century Anglo-India and was used as "baby talk" with children at meal times. Pish-Pash can be prepared with either small pieces of chicken / beef / lamb or mutton or minced meat. If desired the meat could be substituted for green gram dhal or rent lentil dhal. Since Pish-Pash Rice is easily digestible it is good for invalids and little children.

Serves 6   Time required: 1 hour

Ingredients
2 cups raw rice (wash and drain)
250 grams meat (beef, mutton, lamb or chicken)
1 teaspoon whole pepper corns
1 small piece of cinamon
½ teaspoon chopped ginger
Salt to taste
1tablespoon butter or ghee
A few mint leaves

Chop the meat into very small pieces or use minced meat.
Heat oil in a pan and fry the pepper corns, cinamon and chopped ginger for 2 minutes. Add the washed raw rice and meat and stir-fry for a few minutes. Now add the mint, salt and 6 or 7 cups of water and mix well. Cover the pan with a tight fitting lid and simmer on low heat till the rice and meat are very soft. Serve with omelet and pickle.

4. SIMPLE BEEF PALAU / PILAF

This is a simple and popular Anglo-Indian Rice dish that is invariably cooked on Sundays or festive occasions. Tender beef morsels cut mostly from the tenderloin in small steak cubes (with a little fat) is first marinated for a few hours or overnight, then cooked in a slightly spicy gravy to which the Rice is added and simmered till a rich and aromatic Rice dish is obtained.

Serves 6   Time required: 1 hour 20 minutes

Ingredients
2 cups Basmati rice or any other long grained rice
1 Kg Beef Tenderloin (with a little fat) cut into medium size cubes
1 cup oil or ghee
2 teaspoons chillie powder
3 big onions sliced finely
3 or 4 green chilies sliced lengthwise
2 tablespoons ginger garlic paste
3 big tomatoes chopped
1 pack coconut milk
½ cup fresh mint leaves (chopped)
½ cup coriander leaves (chopped)
1 cup curds (yogurt)
½ teaspoon turmeric powder
2 bay leaves
4 cloves, 3 small sticks of cinnamon, 4 cardamoms
Salt to taste

Wash the Beef pieces and marinate with the garam masala / all spice powder, green chillies, curds / yogurt, half the quantity of ginger garlic paste and turmeric powder for about 2 hours.(you could marinate and keep over night if desired)

Heat the oil or ghee in a large vessel or pressure cooker and add the bay leaves, cloves, cinnamon, cardamom, remaining ginger garlic paste and onions and sauté for some time. Add the chopped tomatoes, mint leaves and chillie powder and fry on low heat till the oil separates from the mixture and the tomatoes are reduced to pulp. Add the marinated meat, coconut milk and salt and pressure cook for about 15 minutes till the tender. When the pressure dies down, open the cooker and remove the cooked beef pieces and keep aside.
Now add sufficient water to the left over gravy in the pressure cooker so as to get about 8 glasses of watery gravy. Add the washed rice and cook till half done (without closing the pressure cooker).

Now add the cooked meat and mix well. Cover the pressure cooker with the lid but don't use the weight and cook on low heat for a few more minutes till all the liquid evaporates and the Palau is done.

Let the Palau stand for about 15 minutes before serving with curd chutney or any curry.

5. MUTTON / LAMB PALAU / PILAF

Serves 6   Time required: 1 hour

Ingredients
1 kg Basmati Rice or any other Good Rice ... wash and soak for about 1 hour
1 kg Mutton / Lamb cut into fairly big pieces
3 bay leaves
2 teaspoons all spice powder or garam masala
3 large tomatoes chopped
3 small sticks of cinnamon, 3 cloves, 3 cardamoms
1 cup oil or ghee
Salt to taste
6 green chilies slit lengthwise
3 tablespoons ginger garlic paste
2 teaspoons chillie powder
3 large onions sliced finely
1 teaspoon turmeric powder
½ cup fresh mint leaves
3 tablespoons curds / yogurt

Marinate the mutton / lamb with the garam masala / all spice powder, green chillies, curds / yogurt, half the quantity of ginger garlic paste and turmeric powder for half an hour.

Heat the oil or ghee in a large vessel and add the bay leaves, cloves, cinnamon, cardamom, remaining ginger garlic paste and onions and sauté for some time. Add the chopped tomatoes, mint leaves and chillie powder and simmer till the oil separates from the mixture and the tomatoes are reduced to pulp. Add the marinated mutton / lamb and salt and cook till tender. Remove the pieces and keep aside.

Now add sufficient water to the gravy in the vessel so as to get about 8 glasses of liquid. Add the rice and cook till half done. Now add the cooked mutton / lamb and mix well. Cover and cook on low heat for a few more minutes till all the liquid evaporates and the Rice is done. Let it stand for about 15 minutes before serving with curd chutney or any curry.

6. JUNGLEE CHICKEN PALAU / PILAF

The term 'Junglee' means wild or crazy in Hindi and it also refers to someone or something that is rough round the edges and has no finesse! This rice dish is just that - a mish-mash of ingredients and Spices that are readily available in the kitchen such as onions, tomatoes, chillies, whole spices etc. The recipe varies from person to person. Many choose to incorporate leftover vegetable and meat dishes into it. Each family has their own version of this crazy rice dish or Junglee Palau. This is my version of Junglee Chicken Palau

Serves 6   Time required: 1 hour

Ingredients
2 cups Basmati rice or any other long grained rice
1 Kg chicken chopped into medium size bits
1 cup oil or ghee
2 teaspoons chillie powder
3 big onions sliced finely
3 or 4 green chilies sliced lengthwise
2 tablespoons ginger garlic paste
3 big tomatoes chopped
1 pack coconut milk
½ cup fresh mint leaves
½ cup coriander leaves
1 cup curds (yogurt)
½ teaspoon turmeric powder
2 bay leaves
4 cloves, 3 small sticks of cinnamon, 4 cardamoms
Salt to taste

Wash the rice and soak it in a little water for about 20 minutes.

Heat the ghee in a suitable vessel or rice cooker and add the whole spices and bay leaves and fry for a few minutes. Now add the onions and ginger garlic paste and sauté for some time. Add the turmeric, mint leaves, coriander leaves and chillie powder and fry for a while. Next add the chopped tomatoes and chicken keep on frying till the oil separates from the mixture. Add the curds, slit green chilies, coconut milk and salt and 1 cup of water and simmer for a few minutes till the chicken is tender. Now add the rice and 3 cups of water and cook on low heat till done mixing once or twice. Serve with curd chutney and chicken or meat curry.

7. PRAWN PALAU / PILAF

Serves 6   Time required: 1 hour

Ingredients
2 cups raw rice wash and soak for 20 minutes
½ kg cleaned and de-veined prawns
1-cup coconut paste or 1 cup coconut milk
2 tablespoons ginger garlic paste
2 onions sliced finely
3 green chilies slit lengthwise
A few mint leaves
2 tablespoons coriander leaves
1 teaspoon chillie powder
1 teaspoon spice powder
½ cup oil or ghee
1 teaspoon cumin powder
Salt to taste

Wash the prawns and keep aside.

Heat oil in a vessel and fry the onions till golden brown. Add the ginger garlic paste, green chilies and coriander leaves and sauté for some time. Add the chillie powder, cumin powder, salt and prawns and mix well. Cook for about 5 minutes on low heat till the prawns are cooked. Remove the prawns and keep aside.

Now add the coconut to the gravy in the vessel and mix well. Add 4 cups of water (and a little more salt if required) and bring to boil. Add the rice and mix well. Cover the vessel with a tight fitting lid and cook on low heat till the rice is cooked and all the water dries up. Mix in the prawns and simmer on how heat for another 2 or 3 minutes, then turn off the heat. Let it stand for about 15 minutes before serving. Serve hot with Prawn Vindaloo and a salad.

8. FISH PALAU / PILAF

Serves 6   Time required: 1 hour

Ingredients:
2 cups raw rice (Wash and soak for 20 minutes)
1 kg good fleshy fish cut into thick chunks or fillets
4 tablespoons coconut paste or 1 cup coconut milk
2 tablespoons ginger garlic paste
3 onions sliced finely
4 green chilies slit lengthwise
1 tablespoon chopped mint leaves
2 tablespoons coriander leaves
1 teaspoon chillie powder
1 teaspoon all spice powder / garam masala powder
½ cup oil
2 tablespoons ghee
1 teaspoon cumin powder
Salt to taste
2 Bay leaves
4 cloves, 2 pieces cinnamon, 3 cardamoms

Wash the fish and marinate it with a 1 teaspoon chillie powder, ½ teaspoon turmeric powder and a pinch of Salt for half an hour. Heat 2 tablespoons oil in a flat non-stick pan and lightly fry the fish till firm. Remove and keep aside.

Heat the remaining oil in a suitable vessel and fry the onions, bay leaves and spices till golden brown. Add the ginger garlic paste, green chilies and coriander leaves and sauté for some time. Add the chillie powder, cumin powder, salt and coconut and mix well. Fry till the oil separates from the mixture. Add 4 cups of water and bring to boil. Now add the rice and mix well. Cook on low heat till most of the water has been absorbed. Mix in the fried fish gently. Simmer till the rice is cooked and all the water dries up. Serve hot with curd and onion chutney.

9. EGG PALAU / PILAF

Serves 6   Time required: 1 hour

Ingredients
3 big onions sliced finely
3 or 4 green chilies sliced lengthwise
2 tablespoons ginger garlic paste
3 big tomatoes chopped
3 tablespoons chopped coriander leaves
1cup curds (yogurt)
1 teaspoon turmeric powder
2 bay leaves
4 cloves, 4 pieces of cinnamon, 4 cardamoms
Salt to taste
10 Eggs boiled and shelled
½ kg Biryani rice or Basmati rice
4 tablespoons oil
2 tablespoons ghee
2 teaspoons chillie powder

Wash the rice and soak it in a little water for about 20 minutes.
Heat the oil and ghee in a suitable vessel or rice cooker and add the whole spices and bay leaves and fry for a few minutes. Now add the onions, ginger garlic paste and sauté for some time. Add the boiled eggs, turmeric powder, coriander leaves and chillie powder and fry for a while. Next add the chopped tomatoes and salt and keep on frying till the oil separates from the mixture. Add the curds, slit green chilies and salt and simmer for 10 to 15 minutes. Add 3 cups of water and bring to boil. Now add the rice and cook on low heat till done, mixing once or twice. Serve with curd chutney and chicken or meat curry.

10. MIXED VEGETABLE PALAU / PILAF

Serves 6   Time required: 45 minutes

Ingredients
2 cups basmati rice or any other raw rice
2 cups assorted vegetables such as carrots, beans, peas, cauliflower etc cut into medium size bits
3 onions sliced finely,
1 cup ground coconut
½ teaspoon turmeric powder
2 teaspoons ginger garlic paste
½ cup oil or ghee
Salt to taste
3 green chilies chopped
2 teaspoons chillie powder
2 Bay leaves
4 cloves, 2 pieces cinnamon, 3 cardamoms

Heat oil in a suitable vessel or cooker and fry the onions, bay leaf and whole spices till brown. Add the ginger garlic paste and green chilies and sauté for a few minutes. Add the chopped vegetables, chillie powder, turmeric powder and salt and stir-fry for a few minutes. Add the coconut and fry till the oil separates from the mixture. Add 4 cups of water and bring to boil. Add the rice and mix well. Cook on medium heat till the rice is cooked and each grain is separate. Garnish with chopped coriander leaves.

11. FISH AND BOILED EGGS KEDGEREE

Kedgeree is a mildly spiced rice and lentil mix-up which originated during the time of the British Raj. It is the anglicized version of the Indian Rice dish Kichiri or Kichadi. It was originally prepared with fillets or flakes of steamed or smoked haddock (but later salmon, kippers or tuna was used instead) parsely, boiled eggs, nuts, sultanas, rice and lentils. It made a hearty breakfast dish in the early days when it was considered healthy to have a cooked breakfast with all the essential nutrients.

Serves 6   Time required: 45 minutes

Ingredients
½ kg good fleshy fish cut into thick fillets
2 cups raw rice or Basmati Rice
4 tablespoons oil
1 tablespoon ghee or butter
3 onions sliced finely
3 green chillies sliced lengthwise
4 tablespoons Red Lentil Dal / Masoor dhal (Or any other lentils)
3 cloves
2 small sticks of cinnamon
1 teaspoon cumin powder
100 grams Sultanas or Raisins (Optional)
3 tablespoons chopped coriander leaves
2 Bay leaves
Salt to taste
1 teaspoon chillie powder
1 tablespoon lime juice / lemon juice / vinegar
6 whole peppercorns
4 hard-boiled eggs cut into quarters.

Cook the fish in a little water along with the Bay leaves and salt for about 5 minutes or till the pieces are firm. Remove the boiled fish and keep aside.
Add sufficient water to the left over fish soup / stock to get 6 cups of liquid and keep aside.
Remove the bones and skin from the boiled fish and break into small pieces. Wash the Rice and dhal and keep aside.
Heat the oil in a suitable vessel and sauté the onions, cloves and cinnamon lightly. Add the slit green chillies, whole peppercorns, cumin powder and chillie powder and sauté for a few minutes. Add the rice and dhal and mix well. Now add 6 cups of the fish soup / stock, lime juice / vinegar, sultanas, chopped coriander leaves and salt and cook on high heat till boiling. Reduce heat and simmer covered till the rice and dhal are cooked and slightly pasty. Gently mix in the cooked fish, butter / ghee and the hard-boiled eggs. Cover and let the rice draw in the fish for a few minutes. Serve hot or cold with Chutney or Lime Pickle.

12. GOOD FRIDAY RICE CONGEE / GRUEL

Serves 6   Time required: 1 hour

Ingredients
½ cup Raw Rice
½ cup Moong Dhal (Split Green gram dhal)
¼ cup Brown Sugar or Jaggery
½ cup grated coconut or 1 cup coconut milk
2 tablespoons raisins
A pinch of salt

Wash the rice and soak it for half an hour in a little water. Dry roast the Moong Dhal lightly in a pan and take down. Heat 3 cups of water and the salt in a vessel, and when nicely boiling add the rice and the roasted Moong Dhal. Cook on low heat till the rice and dhal are soft and mushy. Add the coconut, sugar/ jaggery and raisins and mix well. Simmer for 2 or 3 minutes, then turn off the heat. The Congee should be of the consistency of thick soup.
Serve plain or with Coconut chutney either hot or cold

(Omit the Brown sugar or jaggery if you want it plain not sweet) This Congee is usually eaten on Good Frid

VI

ANGLO-INDIAN
PICKLES, RELISHES,
CHUTNEYS & SAUCES

Pickles, Relishes and Chutneys add zest to a meal and Anglo-Indian Cuisine has many of them in its repertoire. Pickles and chutneys form an important and sometimes necessary accompaniment to any meal. They add sparkle and tingle to enliven up the meal and they stimulate the appetite with their tangy and spicy flavour.

The secret of a good pickle is the combination of spices such as chillies, fenugreek and mustard either crushed or ground. Pickles are generally made in summer since they should be kept in the sun for some time. Unlike chutneys pickles have a longer shelf life and can be stored for more than a year without spoiling.

1. BRINJAL PICKLE (AUBERGINE / EGG PLANT PICKLE)

Ingredients
1 kg long purple or green Brinjals or 1 large seedless one
3 tablespoons chillie powder
2 tablespoons chopped garlic
2 tablespoons chopped fresh ginger
1 cup vinegar
1 tablespoon mustard powder
1 tablespoon cumin powder
1 teaspoon turmeric powder
1 cup Sesame oil refined oil
1 cup of sugar
2 tablespoons salt

Wash and dry the Brinjals well and cut them into medium size pieces. Heat the oil in a pan. Add the ginger and garlic and sauté on low heat for a few minutes. Add the chillie powder, mustard powder, cumin powder, and turmeric powder and fry for a minute. Now add the Brinjals and salt and cook for 5 to 6 minutes on low heat. Add the vinegar and sugar and mix well. Cook till the sugar dissolves and till the brinjals are just cooked. Cool and store in bottles.

2. MANGO PICKLE (SWEET)

Ingredients
6 medium sized mangoes
3 tablespoons chillie powder
1 tablespoon fenugreek seeds ground coarsely
½ teaspoon turmeric powder
4 tablespoons salt
1 tablespoon mustard powder
1 cup Sesame oil or refined oil
½ cup vinegar
½ cup sugar

Wash and dry the mangoes well. Cut them into medium size pieces. Throw away the seeds. Mix the mango pieces with the turmeric, chillie powder, salt, fenugreek powder, mustard powder, sugar and vinegar in a stone jar and leave in the sun for a week. Shake the jar everyday so that all the mango pieces soak well. After a week, heat the oil in a pan till smoky. Cool and pour over the pickle in the jar. Mix well. The pickle is now ready for use.

3 LIME PICKLE (SWEET)

Ingredients
20 medium sized limes
1 cup of sugar
3 tablespoons chillie powder
3 tablespoons salt
1 teaspoon mustard powder
½ teaspoon powdered fenugreek seeds
½ cup of vinegar
3 tablespoons oil

Cut each lime into 6 or 8 pieces, keeping 6 aside to squeeze out the juice. Steam the limes in hot water for 5 minutes till slightly soft. Dry and Cool for some time. Now mix all the ingredients, and the juice of 6 limes with the steamed lime pieces in a pickle jar. Mix well and leave in the sun for a week. The changed appearance of the limes will show that the pickle is ready for use.

4. GOOSE BERRY PICKLE

Ingredients
½ kg Goose Berries (Star Variety)
2 tablespoons chillie powder
½ teaspoon turmeric powder
1 teaspoon cumin powder
2 tablespoons salt
2 tablespoons vinegar
1 tablespoons sugar

Wash the gooseberries and dry them well. Soak them with salt and leave them in the sun for about 2 hours each day for a week. When the gooseberries shrivel up and change colour add the chillie powder, cumin powder, turmeric powder, vinegar and sugar and mix well. Use when required.

5. CHICKEN PICKLE

Ingredients
2 kg chicken chopped into tiny pieces
100 grams garlic
100 grams ginger
50 grams red chilies
2 tablespoons mustard powder
1 teaspoon powdered fenugreek seeds
3 cups vinegar
½ kg refined oil or Sesame oil
½ cup salt

Make a paste of the garlic, ginger, and red chilies with a little vinegar. Wash the chicken well and wipe dry. Heat oil in a suitable pan and fry the ground masala paste on low heat for about 3 minutes. Add the chicken pieces and mix well. Simmer for 5 minutes. Add the rest of the vinegar, salt, mustard powder and fenugreek powder and cook on low heat till the chicken is tender and all the gravy dries up. Simmer till the oil floats on top. Cool and store in bottles.
This pickle will last for a month and can be had with rice, chapattis or bread. (This Pickle should be kept in the fridge).

6. FISH PADDA (FISH PICKLE)

Ingredients
500 grams sardines or small mackerels or any other small fish cut into fairly big pieces
3 tablespoons chopped garlic
2 tablespoons chopped ginger
3 tablespoons chillie powder

2 teaspoons garlic paste
1 tablespoon cumin powder
½ teaspoon turmeric powder
1 teaspoon mustard powder
2 teacups vinegar
20 or 25 curry leaves
½ liter sesame oil or mustard oil
Salt to taste

Marinate the fish with turmeric powder & salt for half an hour. Fry the fish lightly in either sesame oil or mustard oil, for 5-8 minutes. It should only be slightly crisp. Remove & keep aside.

In the same oil add the curry leaves, chopped ginger and garlic and fry for a few minutes. Mix in the garlic paste, chillie powder, cumin powder, mustard powder and salt and fry with a little vinegar till the oil separates from the mixtures and gives out a nice aroma. Add the rest of the vinegar and the fried fish and mix well. Simmer for 2 more minutes then take down.
Cool and store in bottles. This pickle will last for about 6 months if stored in the fridge.

Note; Instead of fresh fish, Salt fish can be used instead.

7. SALT FISH PICKLE

Ingredients
½ kg good salt fish cut into small bits
3 tablespoons chillie powder
½ teaspoon tumeric powder
1 teaspoon mustard powder
1 teaspoon cumin powder
¼ teaspoon nutmeg powder
1 tablespoon sliced ginger pieces
1 tablespoon sliced garlic pieces
2 tablespoons salt
1 cup Sesame oil (Til oil)

1 cup vinegar
1 teaspoon fenugreek seeds

Wash the salt fish well and leave to dry for some time. Smear the turmeric powder on the salt fish. Heat 2 tablespoons oil in a pan and fry the salt fish till golden brown. Keep aside. In another pan heat the remaining oil till smoky, then turn off the heat. Add all the other ingredients and the fried salt fish and mix well. Store in bottles when cold. This pickle need not be stored in a fridge.

8. PRAWN PICKLE

Ingredients
200 grams dried prawns
2 tablespoons chillie powder
½ teaspoon turmeric powder
1 tablespoon chopped garlic
2 tablespoons salt
1 teaspoon powdered mustard seeds
1 teaspoon powdered fenugreek seeds
A few curry leaves
1 cup sunflower oil or sesame oil
1 cup vinegar

Wash the prawns well and leave to dry in the sun for one hour.
Heat 2 tablespoons oil in a pan and fry the prawns till brown. Keep aside. In another pan heat the remaining oil till smoky. Add the curry leaves and chopped garlic and fry well. Now add the chillie powder, fenugreek seeds powder, mustard powder, salt and vinegar and fry for some time. Add the prawns and mix well. Simmer for 5 minutes then remove from heat. When the pickle is cold, store in bottles and use when required.

9. PORK PICKLE

Ingredients
½ kg boneless pork preferably without fat, cut into small bits
3 tablespoons chillie powder
½ teaspoon turmeric powder
2 teaspoons cumin powder
½ teaspoon nutmeg powder
1 teaspoon all spice powder
1 tablespoon chopped garlic
1 teaspoon chopped ginger
2 tablespoons salt
1 cup Refined Oil or Sesame oil
2 cups vinegar

Wash the pork well and leave to dry for some time.
Heat the oil in a pan and sauté the garlic and ginger for some time. Add the pork and fry on high heat till the pork pieces turn firm. Add the chillie powder, cumin powder, nutmeg powder, spice powder, turmeric, vinegar and salt and mix well. Cook on low heat without adding water, till the pork is cooked and the gravy is almost dry. Remove from heat and cool. When completely cold, store in bottles and use when required. This pickle should be kept in the fridge

10 MEAT PICKLE

Ingredients
½ kg boneless meat either beef or mutton cut into small bits
3 tablespoons chillie powder
½ teaspoon turmeric powder
2 teaspoons cumin powder
½ teaspoon nutmeg powder
1 teaspoon all spice powder
2 tablespoons chopped garlic
1 teaspoon chopped ginger
2 tablespoons salt
1 cup Refined Oil or Sesame oil
2 cups vinegar

Wash the meat well and leave to dry. Heat the oil in a pan and sauté the garlic and ginger for some time. Add the meat and fry on high heat till the pork pieces turn firm. Add chillie powder, cumin powder, nutmeg powder, spice powder, turmeric, vinegar and salt and mix well. Cook on low heat till the meat is cooked and the gravy is almost dry. Remove from heat and cool. When completely cold, store in Bottles and use when required (keep in the fridge).

11 SWEET MANGO CHUTNEY PRESERVE
A sweet and sour Pickled Preserve made with semi ripe Polly mangoes and spices. A good relish with any Anglo-Indian Curry and it could also be used while making Meat Glassy. Real competition to Crosse and Blackwell's Major Grey's Mango Chutney

Ingredients
4 semi raw Mangoes (Polly Mangoes)
1 cup vinegar
1 cup sugar
2 tablespoons chillie powder
1 tablespoon chopped garlic
1 tablespoon chopped ginger
2 tablespoons salt
100 grams raisins
2 small sticks of cinnamon

Wash the mangoes and dry them well. Peel the skins and grate the mangoes. Discard the seeds. Cook the grated mango with the cinnamon, raisins, vinegar and sugar and cook on low heat till soft. Add all the remaining ingredients and mix well. Simmer for 5 more minutes then remove from heat. Cool and store in bottles.

12. DEVIL CHUTNEY (HELL'S FLAME CHUTNEY)
Devil Chutney is a fiery red chutney. Its bright red colour often leads people to think that is very pungent and spicy, when actually it is sweetish and only slightly pungent The vinegar and sugar react with the onion

and red chilly to produce the bright red colour. It is also known as HELL FIRE OR HELL'S FLAME CHUTNEY due to its vivid colour.

Ingredients
1 medium size onion chopped roughly
1 teaspoon raisins (optional)
½ teaspoon red chillie powder
2 teaspoons sugar
A pinch of salt
2 tablespoons vinegar

Grind all the above ingredients together till smooth. If chutney is too thick add a little more vinegar. Serve with Coconut Rice.

13. PALAU CHUTNEY - CURD / YOGURT CHUTNEY

Ingredients
2 tablespoons roughly ground coconut paste
2 green chilies
2 medium size onions chopped finely
1 tablespoon chopped coriander leaves
½ teaspoon salt
1 teaspoon lime juice
½ teaspoon sugar
½ cup curds or yogurt

Mix all the ingredients together and serve as an accompaniment for Biryani or Palau.

14. TOMATO CHUTNEY

Ingredients
2 big tomatoes chopped
3 green chilies chopped
½ teaspoon cumin powder
1 tablespoon chopped garlic
1 medium size onion chopped

Salt to taste
A pinch of sugar

Heat oil in a pan and fry the onions and garlic for a few minutes. Add the chopped tomatoes, cumin powder, salt, sugar and green chilies and fry till the tomatoes are reduced to a pulp. Grind in a blender. Season with mustard seeds, red chilies and curry leaves.

15. MINT CHUTNEY

Ingredients
1 cup mint leaves
½ cup coriander leaves
3 green chilies
A small ball of tamarind
A small piece of ginger
1 tablespoon sugar
½ teaspoon salt

Grind all the ingredients together till smooth.
Serve with rice, chapattis or as a sandwich paste.

16. CORIANDER AND COCONUT CHUTNEY

Ingredients
4 tablespoons fresh grated coconut or desiccated coconut
1 small bunch fresh coriander leaves
Salt to taste
1 green chillie
½ teaspoon grated ginger
1 teaspoon lemon juice

Grind all the above ingredients together with a little water in a blender till smooth. Add a little more water if a thinner consistency is required. This chutney can be served as an accompaniment with any savoury dish.

17. ONION AND TOMATO SAMBAL

Ingredients
1 big tomato
1 teaspoon chillie powder
1 green chillie
3 flakes garlic chopped
3 medium size onions chopped
Salt to taste
A pinch of sugar

Wash and chop the tomato. Heat oil in a pan and fry the onions and chopped garlic for a few minutes. Add the chopped tomato, chillie powder, salt, sugar and green chilie and fry for a few more minutes till the tomato is pulpy and the Sambal is quite thick.

18. SWEET MANGO CHUTNEY

Ingredients
1 half ripe Polly mango or any other variety skinned and cut into small pieces
1 tablespoon vinegar
2 tablespoons sugar
Salt to taste
1 teaspoon chopped ginger
20 grams raisins

Grind all the above ingredients together to a smooth paste. Serve with savoury fritters or Somasas.

19. PEANUT CHUTNEY / DIP

Ingredients
½ cup roasted peanuts / ground nuts
2 dry red chilies
½ teaspoon salt

1 teaspoon sugar
1 tablespoon vinegar

Grind all the above to a smooth paste in a blender. Serve with any savoury dish.

20. WHITE SAUCE

Ingredients
3 tablespoons flour
1 cup milk
1 tablespoon butter
½ teaspoon pepper
½ teaspoon salt

Warm the milk with a little water in a pan. Mix in the flour and stir to get a smooth paste. Add the butter, pepper powder and salt and mix well. Cook for 3 or 4 more minutes on low heat till the mixture thickens, then turn off the heat. This sauce can be used for any dish calling for white sauce

21. BROWN SAUCE

Ingredients
3 carrots peeled and chopped
2 medium size onions chopped
2 bay leaves
1 teaspoon chopped mint
2 tablespoons tomato puree or finely chopped tomatoes
2 tablespoons butter
2 tablespoons flour
1 teaspoon pepper powder
1 teaspoon salt

Cook the carrots along with the bay leaves, mint and 1 cup of water till they are soft. Mash well and strain so that you get a smooth paste. Throw away the residue. Melt the butter in a pan and stir in the flour. Simmer for a few seconds. Remove from heat and mix in the tomato, carrot stock, pepper and salt. Mix well. Simmer on low heat for 2 or 3 minutes till the sauce thickens a little, then remove from heat. This sauce can be used for any dish calling for a brown sauce.

22. CHEESE SAUCE

Ingredients
½ cup milk
1 tablespoon butter
1 tablespoon flour
3 tablespoons grated cheese
½ teaspoon white pepper powder

Warm the milk with a little water in a pan. Mix in the flour and stir to get a smooth paste
Add the butter, grated cheese, pepper powder and salt and mix well. Cook for 3 or 4 more minutes on low heat till the mixture thickens, then turn off the heat. Serve with any baked dish.

23. HOME MADE MAYONNAISE

Ingredients
2 eggs
1 cup salad oil
1 tbsp vinegar
2 tbsp sugar
1 tsp pepper

Blend the eggs in a blender and add the salad oil, sugar and pepper very slowly, pouring the oil in a thin line. Keep blending till the right consistency is reached.
Use as a salad dressing, in sandwiches, burgers etc.

24. HOMEMADE SANDWICH PASTE

Ingredients:
200 grams minced meat
1 tomato chopped
1 onion chopped
1 green chillie chopped
1 teaspoon pepper powder
½ teaspoon chillie powder
1 teaspoon chopped garlic
Salt to taste
1 teaspoon chopped mint

In a pan add the mince, garlic, onions, green chillie, pepper powder, chillie powder and salt with a little water and cook till the mince is dry. Remove from heat and cool for some time. When cold, blend in a mixer till smooth.

25. HOMEMADE COUNTRY MUSTARD SAUCE

Ingredients
50 grams ordinary black or brown mustard
10 grams white mustard
1 teaspoon chillie powder
2 teaspoons garlic paste
2 tablespoons sugar
Salt to taste
A small piece of Drumstick Bark
1 cup white vinegar
Grind all the above to a smooth paste. Add a little more vinegar to make the paste into a sauce like consistency. Refrigerate and use when required.

Note: In case the drumstick bark is not available substitute with a stick of cinnamon.

VII

ANGLO-INDIAN ROASTS, BAKES & CASSEROLES

This section focuses more on the 'Anglo' part of Anglo-Indian Cuisine where the focus is on cooking simple and easy one dish meals in an oven. The selection of recipes covers a variety of easy to make Anglo-Indian Roasts, Casseroles and Baked dishes. Whether cooking an everyday meal, or for festive occasions, the easy-to-follow directions make cooking these dishes simple and problem-free. The process of preparation and cooking has been simplified, while only easily available ingredients are made use of.

1. ROASTED WHOLE PEPPER CHICKEN

Serves: 6   Time required: 1 hour 15 minutes.

Ingredients
1 whole chicken cleaned and washed well
Salt to taste
4 teaspoons ground black pepper / pepper powder
3 tablespoons oil or butter
2 whole onions pealed
1 teaspoon whole pepper corns
2 one inch pieces of cinnamon
3 potatoes peeled and cut in halves

Preheat oven to 200 Degrees C
Marinate the chicken with the salt and pepper for about ½ an hour. Heat oil or butter in a thick-bottomed pan and add the whole chicken and onion. Turn the chicken from side to side and fry for about for about 5 minutes. Transfer to an ovenproof dish. Place the potatoes around the chicken. Bake in a moderate oven (180 Degrees C) till the chicken is roasted to a lovely golden brown. Serve with roasted potatoes and boiled vegetables.

2. WHOLE DUCK ROASTED THE ANGLO-INDIAN WAY

Serves: 6   Time required: 1 hour 45 minutes.

Ingredients
1 whole duck with the skin
1 tablespoon garlic chopped very finely
1 teaspoon chopped ginger
2 teaspoons ground black pepper / pepper powder
Salt to taste
2 teaspoons lime juice
2 tablespoons oil
1 tablespoon butter

Preheat oven to 200 Degrees C

Heat the oil in a big pan or pressure cooker and sear the duck together with the chopped ginger and garlic till it changes colour to a light brown.

Add the pepper powder, salt, lime juice and 2 or 3 cups of water and cook till the duck is tender. Transfer to a baking dish. Add a tablespoon of butter or ghee and bake in a moderate oven till the duck is nicely browned. Serve hot or cold with boiled vegetables and mash potato

3. ROASTED STUFFED TURKEY

Serves: 6   Time required: 2 hours 45 minutes.

Ingredients
1 Whole small dressed Turkey
¼ cup vinegar
3 teaspoons ground black pepper / pepper powder
2 cups bread crumbs
2 teaspoons chopped fresh mint or dried mint
2 eggs beaten
1 cup of boiled peas and carrot
½ teaspoon grated lemon rind
½ cup oil
Salt to taste

Preheat oven to 200 Degrees C

Rub the turkey with a little salt and pepper and keep aside.

Cook all the innards of the turkey such as liver, heart, gizzards and other edible internal parts of the turkey with a little water, salt and pepper powder till soft. Remove and chop into very tiny bits. This is known as the Turkey Giblets mince.

Mix the cooked giblet mince with the eggs, bread crumbs, vinegar, mint, lemon rind, salt and the boiled carrots and peas.

Now slit the turkey near the neck just above the chest and fill it well with the giblet mince mixture packing it firmly and tightly. When the turkey is stuffed well, close the opening and rub oil well all over it. Tie the legs of the turkey with a bit of string. Place the stuffed turkey in a large ovenproof dish and add sufficient water. Cover with aluminum foil. Bake in a moderate oven oven (180 Degrees C) for 2 hours till the turkey is tender. Remove the foil and roast for some more time till the turkey turns a lovely golden brown all over.

Serve hot or cold with boiled veggies and mash potatoes and Bread.

4. SPICY BEEF ROAST

Serves: 6   Time required: 1 hour 45 minutes.

Ingredients
2 kg Beef from the "Round Portion" or "Top Rump part"
2 large onions cut into quarters
2 teaspoons ground black pepper / pepper powder
2 teaspoons chillie powder
Salt to taste
3 tablespoons oil
3 large potatoes pealed

Preheat oven to 200 Degrees C
Wash the meat and rub the salt and pepper well into it. Place it in a big pan or a pressure cooker, and sear on high heat for a few minutes. Keep turning the meat on all sides till it changes colour.
Add the onions, potatoes and sufficient water and cook till the meat is tender. Transfer to an oven proof dish and bake in a moderate oven oven (180 Degrees C) till the meat is nicely brown all over and the potatoes too are well roasted. Serve hot or cold with bread

5. Oven Pot Roast Meat

Serves: 6   Time required: 1 hour 30 minutes

Ingredients
2 kg chunk of either tender Beef / Mutton / Lamb
2 teaspoons flour (maida)
2 teaspoons ground black pepper / pepper powder
1 teaspoon salt

2 teaspoons vinegar
4 tablespoons butter
2 big onions sliced
3 large potatoes peeled and cut into halves

Preheat oven to 200 Degrees C
Rinse the meat and rub the flour, salt, pepper and vinegar well into it all over. Heat a large ovenproof pan and add the butter. Place the meat in this and brown all over, turning it from side to side. Turn off the heat. Arrange the potatoes and onions around the meat. Add 1 cup of water and cover the dish with a lid or with foil. Roast in a moderate oven (180 Degrees C), for about one hour, or till the meat is cooked and well browned. Serve hot or cold with steamed vegetables and bread.

6. ROAST WHOLE LEG OF LAMB

Serves: 6   Time required: 2 Hours.

Ingredients
1 whole leg of lamb
3 large potatoes
1 tablespoon vinegar
2 teaspoons ground black pepper / pepper powder
4 large onions each chopped into 4 pieces
2 red chillies broken into bits
2 cloves and 2 pieces of cinamon
Salt to taste
3 tablespoons oil

Preheat oven to 200 Degrees C
Wash the mutton leg and make deep cuts on it. Rub it well all over with the salt, pepper and vinegar. Place it in a big baking pan. Add the potatoes, onions, red chillies, cinamon, cloves, oil and sufficient water. Cover with aluminum foil and bake in a moderate oven (180 Degrees C) for about 1 hour 15 minutes or till the meat is tender.

Remove the foil and continue roasting till the meat is nice and brown and the potatoes too are roasted well. Serve hot or cold with bread or with spiced rice.

7. SIMPLE ANGLO-INDIAN PORK ROAST

Serves: 6   Time required: 1 hour 20 minutes

Ingredients
2 kg chunk of pork tender loin
2 teaspoons refined flour (maida)
2 teaspoons ground black pepper / pepper powder
1 teaspoon salt
2 teaspoons vinegar
4 tablespoons butter
2 big onions sliced
3 large potatoes peeled and cut into halves

Preheat oven to 200 Degrees C
Rinse the pork and rub the flour, salt, pepper and vinegar well into it all over. Heat a large ovenproof pan and add the butter. Place the onions and pork in this and brown all over, turning it from side to side. Remove from heat and arrange the potatoes around the pork. Add 2 cups of water and cover the dish with a lid or with foil. Cook in a moderate oven (180 Degrees C) for about one hour or till the meat is cooked and browned well. Serve hot or cold with steamed vegetables and bread.

8. ROASTED PORK SPARE RIBS

Serves: 6   Time required: 1 hour 30 minutes

Ingredients
750 grams Pork spare ribs or tender pork chops
3 medium size carrots
2 tablespoons butter
1 teaspoon dried herbs or dried mint
2 large onions sliced finely

2 teaspoons ground black pepper / pepper powder
1 teaspoon ginger garlic paste
2 tablespoons flour
2 cups water
Salt to taste

Preheat oven to 200 Degrees C
Heat the butter in a pan and brown the pork spare ribs on all sides, then remove and keep aside. In the same pan sauté the onions and ginger garlic paste for some time. Add the flour and mix well. Slowly add one cup of water stirring all the time. Add the pepper powder, dried herbs / mint and salt and some more water and cook on low heat for 5 minutes till the meat is cooked and the water reduces. Place the pork ribs in a buttered casserole dish and pour the contents of the pan over the spare ribs. Arrange the carrots on top and cover with foil. Now cook in a moderate oven (180 Degrees C) for about 45 minutes.
Serve with bread and steamed vegetables.

9. BAKED BEEF STEAKS

Serves: 6   Time required: 1 hour excluding the marinating time

Ingredients
1 kg Beef Undercut cut into steaks
1 teaspoon turmeric powder
4 teaspoons fresh ground black pepper / pepper powder
3 tablespoons oil
2 big onions sliced finely
2 big tomatoes chopped
Salt to taste
3 large potatoes cut into quarters

Preheat oven to 200 Degrees C
Marinate the Steaks with the pepper powder, salt and turmeric powder in a flat plate. Pour the oil on top and keep it over night in the refrigerator (or for at least 4 hours before cooking), Remove from the refrigerator and add the onions and tomatoes and mix well.

Transfer to an oven-proof dish. Arrange the potatoes at the side. Cook in a moderate oven (180 Degrees C) for about 45 minutes to one hour or till the steaks and the potatoes are tender and a brown colour. Serve hot with steamed vegetables and bread.

10. SIMPLE BAKED MUTTON / LAMB CHOPS

Serves: 6   Time required: 1 hour

Ingredients
8 to 10 tender lamb chops
3 potatoes peeled and halved
2 tablespoons oil
2 teaspoons vinegar
1 teaspoon ginger garlic paste
1 teaspoon ground black pepper / pepper powder
Salt to taste

Preheat oven to 200 Degrees C
Marinate the chops with the vinegar, ginger garlic paste, pepper powder and salt for about 2 hours. Arrange the marinated chops in a buttered flat ovenproof dish. Arrange the potatoes around. Pour oil on top. Sprinkle a little salt and pepper powder on the potatoes. Bake in a moderate oven (180 Degrees C) for 30 minutes then grill for 5 to 10 minutes to brown the top. Serve with Rice or toast and onion rings.

11. STEAMED MEAT LOAF

Serves: 6   Time required: 1 hour 15 minutes

Ingredients
300 grams fine Beef Mince / ground beef
2 eggs beaten
2 teaspoons mixed herb powder or dried mint
5 tablespoons bread crumbs
1 teaspoon salt
2 teaspoons ground black pepper / pepper powder

2 tablespoons butter
2 tablespoons chopped celery or coriander

Mix the beef mince with the eggs, mixed herbs/ dried mint,
3 tablespoons bread crumbs, salt and pepper. Shape into a roll and
wrap tightly in a greased sheet of aluminum foil. Heat sufficient water
(for steaming) in a suitable pan. When the water boils, place the wrapped
meat loaf in it. Add half a lime or a teaspoon of vinegar in the water while
boiling to prevent the foil from turning black.
Lower the heat and cook on low heat for about 35 minutes.
While the meat loaf is cooking, melt the butter in another pan and add
the remaining breadcrumbs and sauté for 5 minutes. Add the celery /
coriander and a pinch of salt and pepper and mix well.

Remove the meat loaf from the pan of water and when cool, unwrap it.
Roll it in the buttered breadcrumbs mixture. Now place it in a buttered
ovenproof dish and bake in a moderate oven (180 Degrees C) for 10
minutes. Leave it to cool. When cold, slice the meat loaf into thin slices.
Serve with mashed potatoes and a green salad.

12. BAKED MINCE LOAF

Serves: 6   Time required: 1 hour

Ingredients
1 kg mince meat either beef or mutton or lamb
2 big onions chopped
2 tomatoes chopped
1 teaspoon ginger garlic paste
1 teaspoon chopped mint
4 tablespoons bread crumbs
1 egg beaten
Salt to taste
1 cup water
2 chicken soup cubes
1 teaspoon ground black pepper / pepper powder
1 teaspoon chillie powder

Preheat oven to 200 Degrees C

Heat 1 tablespoon oil in a suitable pan and add the mince, onions, ginger garlic paste, tomatoes, soup cubes and a little salt and simmer on low heat till the mince is cooked and the water dries up.

Mix the cooked mince with half the breadcrumbs, pepper, chillie powder, chopped mint and a little more salt if required. Bind stiffly with the beaten egg.

Butter an oblong loaf tin or dish and coat it with the remaining breadcrumbs. Pack in the cooked mince mixture tightly and cover with aluminum foil. Bake in a moderate oven (180 Degrees C) for 40 to 45 minutes. When cold, turn out upside down on to a serving plate. Serve with bread and a green salad.

13. SHEPHERD'S PIE

Serves: 6   Time required: 1 hour

Ingredients
500 grams minced meat
2 large onions chopped
2 carrots peeled and sliced (optional)
3 large potatoes boiled and mashed
1 soup cube either chicken or beef
2 tablespoons butter
3 tablespoons flour
2 tablespoons milk
1 teaspoon ground black pepper / pepper powder
1 teaspoon chopped fresh mint or dry herbs
2 tablespoons grated cheddar cheese
Salt to taste

Preheat oven to 200 Degrees C

Cook the mince, chopped onions and carrots with ½ cup of water for about 10 minutes till the mince is cooked and the water reduces. Add the crumbled soup cube, salt, pepper, and mint / herb powder and mix well. Cover and simmer on low heat for 5 more minutes.

Make a smooth paste with the flour and 4 tablespoons water and add to the meat mixture. Simmer for 3 or 4 minutes until the meat mixture thickens. Season the mashed potato with a little butter, salt and milk. (The mixture should not be too soft).

Transfer the cooked meat mixture to a big ovenproof dish. Spread the mashed potato on top evenly using a fork. Sprinkle grated cheese on the potato layer. Bake in a moderate oven (180 Degrees C) for 15 minutes till the cheese melts and the potatoes turn golden. Serve hot with garlic bread or toast.

14. WASHER MAN'S PIE (LAMB CHOPS & POTATO PIE)

Serves: 6   Time required: 1 hour 15 minutes

Ingredients
6 tender mutton chops from the neck portion
2 teaspoons ground black pepper / pepper powder
Salt to taste
2 tablespoons flour
2 tablespoons Worchester sauce
6 large potatoes
3 tablespoons butter
2 eggs beaten
Salt to taste

Preheat oven to 200 Degrees C
Rinse the chops and rub in the pepper, flour and salt. Heat a tablespoon of butter in a pan and sauté the chops for 10 minutes on low heat turning them over every few minutes so that both sides are brown. Add 1 cup of water and simmer on low heat for 15 minutes.
Stir in the Worchester sauce. Remove from heat and transfer to a large ovenproof dish.
Meanwhile boil the potatoes and mash them well adding a pinch of salt and 2 teaspoons butter. Mix in the beaten eggs and 2 tablespoons flour when the potato mash is a little cold. Cover the cooked chops in the baking dish with it. Brush with a little more butter.
Bake in a moderate oven (180 Degrees C) for about 20 minutes until the potato layer turns golden brown. Serve with rice or Garlic Bread.

15. PORK MINCE PIE

Serves: 6   Time required: 1 hour 15 minutes

Ingredients
300 grams pork Sausage Mince (if not available use plain mince)
2 onions chopped
1 large tomato chopped
1 tablespoon chopped coriander or celery
3 tablespoons milk
1 tablespoon butter
1 teaspoon chopped mint
1 teaspoon pepper powder
1 teaspoon salt
4 tablespoons flour
2 potatoes peeled and sliced

Preheat oven to 200 Degrees C
Cook the sausage mince with the tomato, salt, pepper, onions, coriander / celery and ½ cup of water till the mince is cooked and the water dries up.
Butter an ovenproof dish and fill it with the cooked mince. Place the sliced potatoes on top. Make a light dough with the flour and milk and a pinch of salt. Roll out the dough into a thin sheet and cover the dish completely. Mark the edges with a fork and make a few small holes in the dough to allow the steam to escape. Brush with a beaten egg to give a glaze. Bake in a moderate oven (180 Degrees C) for 15 to 20 minutes or till the top is a nice golden brown. Serve hot with French fries or chips.

16. SAVOURY SAUSAGE PIE

Serves: 6   Time required: 1 hour

Ingredients
750 grams sausages
4 onions sliced
3 big potatoes peeled and sliced
1 teaspoon chopped coriander or celery

1 teaspoon chopped mint
2 tablespoons butter
4 tablespoons flour
4 tablespoons milk
1 teaspoon ground black pepper / pepper powder
Salt to taste

Preheat oven to 200 Degrees C
Melt the butter in a pan and stir fry the onions and potatoes for about 10 minutes. Cut the sausages into fairly big pieces and mix in with the onions and potatoes. Add the pepper and salt and sauté for 5 more minutes. Transfer to an ovenproof dish. Sprinkle the chopped coriander or celery and mint on top. Pour ½ cup of water and shake the dish so that the water seeps to the bottom. Make a light dough with the flour, milk and a pinch of salt. Roll out the dough. Dampen the edges of the dough and cover the contents of the dish with it. Mark the edges with a fork and prick all over to allow the steam to escape. Brush the top with a little milk. Bake in a moderate oven (180 Degrees C) for about 45 minutes. Serve hot with Bread or with rice.

17. FISHERMAN'S PIE (A SIMPLE FISH PIE)

Serves: 6   Time required: 1 hour

Ingredients
500 grams any white flesh fish such as pompfret, seer, cod, etc cut into large pieces
2 cups milk
4 large potatoes boiled and mashed with a little salt and milk
2 tablespoons butter
2 tablespoons plain flour
2 tablespoons chopped mint
1 teaspoon ground black pepper / ground pepper
100 grams grated cheese (any variety)
Salt to taste

Pre -heat oven to 200 C.

Boil the fish in a little water for about 5 to 7 minutes till just cooked. Drain away the water and flake the fish with a fork.

Heat the butter in a pan on low heat and add the flour and milk. Stir constantly to get a smooth, thick paste. Remove from heat and add the flaked fish, chopped mint, pepper and salt and gently mix well..

Grease an oven proof dish and spread a layer of mashed potato. Now add the fish mixture over this layer. Top with the mashed potato and spread evenly. Sprinkle the grated cheese evenly over the potato topping. Cook in a moderate oven for 30-40 minutes (at 180 Degrees C), or until the cheese is bubbling and slightly golden brown. Remove from the oven and leave to cool for 5 to 10 minutes. Serve with fresh steamed vegetables.

18. GRILLED WHOLE FISH

Serves: 6   Time required: 1 hour

Ingredients
3 Medium sized pomfrets or butter fish or cod fish
2 teaspoons chillie powder
1 teaspoon Worcestershire sauce
1 tablespoon vinegar
2 Tablespoons oil
Salt to taste

Preheat oven to 200 Degrees C

Clean the fish well, slit sideways and remove the insides. Then wash well. Mix the chillie powder, salt, Worcestershire sauce and vinegar together and apply this paste all over and inside the fish. Leave aside for 15 minutes. Grease a Baking tray and lay the marinated fish on it. Drizzle the oil all over the fish. Grill in a moderate Oven (180 Degrees C) for 15 minutes. Serve with salad and chips.

19. BAKED FISH WITH CHEESE

Serves: 6   Time required: 1 hour

Ingredients
6 medium sized pieces of any boneless fish
2 teaspoons ground black pepper / pepper powder
3 teaspoons butter
½ teaspoon salt
4 spring onions chopped finely
1 teaspoon lime juice
2 tablespoons grated cheese

Preheat oven to 200 Degrees C
Wash the fish and marinate it with the salt, pepper and limejuice for about 10 minutes. Lay the fish flat in a shallow greased baking dish Sprinkle the chopped spring onions and the grated cheese over the fish and dot all over with the butter. Cover the dish with aluminum foil and bake in a moderate oven (180 Degrees C) for about 25 to 30 minutes. Serve with any sauce and garlic bread.

20. CHEESY POTATO AND PEAS BAKE

Serves: 6   Time required: 1 hour

Ingredients
6 large potatoes
1 cup green peas
1 large onion chopped
2 tablespoons butter
Salt to taste
2 teaspoons ground black pepper / pepper powder
1 teaspoon chopped mint
3 tablespoons grated cheese
1 tablespoon chopped coriander or celery

Preheat oven to 200 Degrees C

Wash and boil the potatoes till soft. Peel and mash well. Blanch the peas in hot water for a couple of minutes and drain

Heat butter in a pan and lightly fry the onions for about 10 minutes. Remove from heat and add the mashed potatoes and peas to it. Mix in the pepper powder, salt and chopped mint. Transfer to a buttered ovenproof dish and sprinkle grated cheese and coriander / celery on top. Bake in a moderate oven (180 Degrees C) for 20 minutes till the cheese melts and turns a light golden brown. Serve with mince and toast.

21. CHEESY CAULIFLOWER BAKE

Serves: 6   Time required: 1 hour 15 minutes

Ingredients

1 medium sized cauliflower cut into big florets

2 eggs beaten well

3 tablespoons butter

4 tablespoons grated cheese

3 tablespoons breadcrumbs

3 tablespoons flour

1 cup milk

1 teaspoon salt

1 teaspoon ground black pepper / pepper powder

Preheat oven to 200 Degrees C

Soak the cauliflower florets in warm salt water for 45 minutes.

Cook the cauliflower florets in boiling water with a pinch of salt for 5 minutes. Drain and keep aside.

Melt the butter in a pan and slowly mix in the flour till smooth. Add the milk slowly to the butter and flour mixture. Mix well and simmer on low heat for 5 minutes. Turn off the heat. Add the salt, pepper, beaten eggs, 2 tablespoons grated cheese and 2 tablespoons of breadcrumbs to this sauce and mix well. Now add the cooked cauliflower and mix thoroughly. Transfer to a buttered baking dish. Mix the remaining breadcrumbs and cheese together and spread evenly on top. Bake in a moderate oven (180 Degrees C) for about 20 to 25 minutes till the top is golden brown. Serve hot with French fries and garlic bread.

22. SPINACH AND CHEESE BAKE

Serves: 6   Time required: 1 hour

Ingredients
200 grams pasta or elbow macaroni
3 tablespoons tomato sauce
1 cup chopped spinach
1 large onion sliced
1 large tomato chopped
1 green chillie chopped
2 tablespoons butter
3 tablespoons flour
1 cup milk
½ cup cream
Salt to taste
1 teaspoon ground black pepper / pepper powder
4 tablespoons grated cheese

Preheat oven to 200 Degrees C
Wash and drain the spinach. Cook it with a pinch of salt for 5 minutes without adding water. Leave aside to cool then puree it. Cook the pasta or macaroni in boiling water till soft. Drain and keep aside.
Heat the butter in a pan and sauté the onions and chopped green chilly for 10 minutes. Add the tomatoes and cook on low heat for 5 more minutes.
Meanwhile mix the flour and milk together till smooth. Add this to the onions and tomatoes and mix well. When the sauce thickens add the salt, pepper, 3 tablespoons grated cheese, tomato sauce, pureed spinach, cream and pasta and mix well.
Remove from heat and transfer to a buttered baking dish Sprinkle the remaining cheese on top. Bake in a moderate oven (180 Degrees C) for 15 to 20 minutes. Serve with toast or garlic bread.

23. MACARONI AND MINCE CASSEROLE

Serves: 6   Time required: 45 minutes

Ingredients:
250 grams elbow macaroni
250 grams mince either beef or mutton
2 small onions chopped
2 tomatoes chopped
2 teaspoons chillie powder
1 teaspoon chopped coriander leaves
Salt to taste
2 tablespoons oil
2 tablespoons grated cheese

Preheat oven to 200 Degrees C
Cook the macaroni in boiling salt water till soft. Drain the hot water, pass cold water over it, then drain and keep aside.
Heat the oil in a pan and sauté the onions till brown. Add the mince, ginger garlic paste, tomatoes, chillie powder, salt and coriander leaves and mix well. Cook on low heat till the mince is cooked and all the water dries up. Now add the cooked macaroni and mix well.
Transfer to a buttered baking dish and spread the grated cheese on top. Bake in a moderate oven (180 Degrees C) for 10 minutes till the cheese melts. Serve with tomato sauce.

24. POTLUCK LAMB / MUTTON CASSEROLE

Serves; 6   Time required: 2 hours 15 minutes

Ingredients
1 kg mutton or lamb from the leg portion cut into small pieces
4 potatoes cut into chunks
4 onions sliced finely
4 carrots peeled and cut into thick slices
3 stalks celery washed and cut into chunks (optional)
2 soup cubes of any flavour
2 teaspoons ground black pepper / pepper powder

1 teaspoon chillie powder
1 teaspoon chopped mint
2 tablespoons oil
Salt to taste

Preheat oven to 200 Degrees C
Place a layer of potatoes in a large buttered baking dish.
Arrange the meat, onions, carrots, and the remaining potatoes in layers. Dissolve the soup cubes in 2 cups of boiling water. Add the chillie powder, salt and pepper to it then pour over the meat and vegetables. Drizzle oil all over the dish. Sprinkle the chopped mint and a few pieces of celery on top. Cover the dish with a lid or with aluminum foil and cook in a moderate oven (180 Degrees C) for about 2 hours till the meat is soft and most of the water has dried up.
Decorate the top with remaining chopped celery. Serve with steamed vegetables and mash potatoes

25. CHICKEN CASSEROLE

Serves: 6   Time required: 1 hour

Ingredients
1 chicken cut into 8 to 10 large pieces
1 cup finely chopped mint leaves
2 teaspoons ginger garlic paste
2 teaspoons lemon juice
1 tablespoon vinegar
1 teaspoon cumin powder
1 teaspoon Worcestershire Sauce
1 teaspoon chillie powder
Salt to taste
2 tablespoons oil

Preheat oven to 200 Degrees C
Mix all the above ingredients together in a bowl and apply the mixture to the chicken pieces. Leave to marinate for 30 minutes.

Transfer to a buttered baking dish. Drizzle oil over the chicken. Cover with aluminum foil. Cook in a moderate oven (180 Degrees C) for 45 minutes. Serve with rice and a fresh vegetable salad

----

VIII

ANGLO-INDIAN DESSERTS, CUSTARDS AND PUDDINGS

'Anglo-Indians are known for their Sweet Tooth'. A bit of this and a bit of that when put together turns out to be a scrumptious dessert which is both mouth watering and tempting to round off a meal. Sweets, Puddings and Custards are the ultimate high lights of Anglo-Indian Cuisine. Anglo-Indian sweets and desserts are a mish mash of both Indian and European tastes taking their origins from all the European invasions in India. Served hot or cold, these desserts will turn an average, every day meal into a feast to remember.

1. SUGARY FRIED PLANTAINS

Serves 6   Time required: 1 hour

Ingredients
6 ripe plantains or bananas
1 egg beaten
3 tablespoons bread crumbs
3 tablespoons ghee
2 tablespoons powdered sugar

Slice each plantain into 2 lengthwise. Brush them lightly with the beaten egg then dredge with the bread crumbs.
Heat the ghee in a pan and shallow fry 2 at a time, till golden brown on both sides. Sprinkle powdered sugar on top. Serve hot.

Note: The fried plantains could be served cold with a scoop of Ice cream as well.

2. PLANTAIN FRITTERS

Serves 6   Time required: 1 hour

Ingredients
1 cup plain flour / maida
½ cup rice flour (optional)
2 tablespoons sugar
3 ripe Plantains preferably the long ripe yellow skin variety with a few spots (not the Kerala Bananas)
1 cup milk
A pinch of salt
½ cup water
½ teaspoon vanilla essence
Oil for frying

Mash the plantains and mix it with all the above ingredients (except the oil) to get a smooth thick batter without lumps. Heat oil in a deep pan till smoky. Drop tablespoons of the batter one at a time into the hot oil.

Fry till golden brown. Serve as a tea time treat or as a Dessert with Ice Cream and Chocolate Cake

3. APPLE FRITTERS

Serves 6   Time required: 1 hour

Ingredients
3 Apples with the skins sliced
200 grams refined flour / maida
½ cup milk
100 grams sugar
A pinch of salt
½ cup water
½ teaspoon vanilla essence
Oil for frying

Mix all the ingredients together (except the oil) to get a smooth thick batter without lumps. Heat oil in a deep pan till smoky. Dip the apple spices in the batter and drop one at a time into the hot oil and fry till golden brown. Serve plain or with Ice Cream

4. BANANA COCONUT FRITTERS

An all time favourite fruit delivered in an enchanting treat - Banana Coconut Fritters combines the lovely taste of Bananas and Coconut which everyone will enjoy!!!!

Serves 6   Time required: 1 hour

Ingredients
200 grams wheat flour
100 grams jaggery (powdered) or soft brown sugar
1 cup grated fresh coconut or 4 tablespoons desiccated coconut
2 eggs beaten
2 ripe bananas mashed well
½ teaspoon salt
oil for frying

Mix all the ingredients together to a thick smooth batter. Heat oil in a deep pan till smoky. Drop a tablespoon of the batter at a time into the hot oil and fry till golden brown.

Serve plain or with Vanilla Ice Cream as a Tea time treat.

5. COMLANGA (A PORTUGUESE RIPE PUMPKIN SWEET)

Serves 6   Time required: 1 hour

Ingredients
1 cup grated white pumpkin
1 cup sugar
1 teaspoon lime juice
½ teaspoon vanilla essence
1 teaspoon ghee
1 cup fresh milk or 3 tablespoons condensed milk

Melt the sugar in a thick pan with ½ cup water till a fairly thick syrup is obtained. Add the grated pumpkin and milk / condensed milk and simmer stirring all the time until the mixture begins to crystallize and looks transparent. Add the essence, limejuice and ghee and mix well. When the mixture starts to leave the sides of the pan, pour out onto a greased plate. Cut into squares when quite cold.

6. VANILLA STEWED FRUIT

Serves 6   Time required: 1 hour

Ingredients
3 cups assorted fruit chopped into 1inch pieces such as mango, pineapple, pear, apple, etc
2 tablespoons Brown sugar
½ teaspoon vanilla essence
1 small piece cinnamon
½ cup water.

Place all the above ingredients in a suitable pan. Simmer on low heat for about 25 to 30 minutes till the fruit softens. Take down and cool. Transfer to a glass dish and leave in the refrigerator. Just before serving add a layer of fresh cream on top. Garnish with chopped cherries and nuts.

7. POACHED PEARS AND APPLES IN RED WINE

Serves 6   Time required: 30 minutes

Ingredients
2 medium size hard pears and 2 apples
3 tablespoons sugar
2 cardamoms
1 piece cinnamon
1 cup of sugar
2 cups of water
1 cup Red Wine or Sherry

Pare the pears and apples, remove the seeds and core and cut each into quarters. Heat 2 cups of water in a pan and add the sugar, cardamoms and cinnamon. Simmer for 5 minutes. Add the cut pears and simmer till the pears are soft. Mix in the wine or Sherry and continue stewing till the fruit is very soft. Remove from heat and cool. Serve with fresh cream or custard.
Note: The same recipe can also be used for Stewed Apples, Stewed Pineapple etc.

8. STEWED APRICOTS IN RUM

Serves 6   Time required: 1 hour

Ingredients
300 grams dried apricots
100 grams sugar
2 tablespoons sliced almonds
4 tablespoons thick cream

Stew the apricots with 3 cups of water till they are soft and pulpy. Remove from heat and remove the seeds. Heat the same water that the apricots were stewed in and add the sugar and Rum. Make a syrup then mix in the mashed apricots. Simmer for 2 more minutes then turn off heat. Transfer to a suitable glass dish. Sprinkle the chopped almonds then drizzle the cream on top. Serve chilled.

9. STEWED APPLES IN BRANDY AND HONEY

Serves 6   Time required: 1 hour

Ingredients
4 apples peeled and chopped into quarters
½ cup honey
2 tablespoons brandy
1 teaspoon lime juice
100 grams raisins
2 cups water
1 cup whipped cream for topping

Cook the apples in 1 cup of water till tender. Remove from heat and transfer the cooked apple to a serving dish. Sprinkle raisins on top. Add the honey to the remaining water in which the apples were cooked and simmer on low flame till it forms a thick syrup. Mix in the brandy and lime juice then pour over the apples and raisins. Chill in the refrigerator. Serve with whipped cream.

10. PLAIN CUSTARD

Serves 6   Time required: 45 minute

Ingredients
2 cups cold milk
4 tablespoons sugar
1 teaspoon corn flour
2 eggs

Separate the egg yolks from the whites and whisk the whites to a stiff froth. Mix the yolks with the cold milk, corn flour and sugar and beat well. Place this mixture on very low heat and stir constantly until it thickens. Do no boil. When the mixture, is sufficiently thick, top with the beaten egg whites and cook for 2 more minutes on low heat without mixing. Cool and serve.

Note: This is a basic custard recipe. Add whatever flavouring is desired and serve with fresh fruit, cake etc

11. CARAMEL CUSTARD

Serves 6   Time required: 1 hour

Ingredients
3 large eggs
2 cups milk
½ cup sugar
½ teaspoon vanilla essence
¼ cup sugar for the caramel

Melt ¼ cup sugar in a saucepan till it caramelizes. Coat the sides of the custard mould with the caramel syrup. Beat the eggs, sugar, milk and essence together and pour the mixture over the caramel. Steam gently for 45 minutes or until the mixture is just firm. Cool and keep aside for one hour. Turnover on a serving dish. Serve plain or with fruit salad.

12. COCONUT CUSTARD

Serves 6   Time required: 1 hour

Ingredients
2 cups Desiccated Coconut
2 Cups milk
4 Eggs
2 Tablespoons sugar

Boil the milk and the desiccated coconut together. Keep aside to cool. Beat the Eggs and the sugar together till frothy then mix in the cold milk and coconut. Mix well. Pour into a custard bowl and steam till the custard is cooked. Serve cold.

13. CHOCOLATE CUSTARD

Serves 6   Time required: 1 hour

Ingredients
2 cups cold milk
5 tablespoons sugar
1 teaspoon corn flour
2 eggs
2 tablespoons cocoa powder

Separate the egg yolks from the whites and whisk the whites to a stiff froth. In a saucepan, mix the yolks with the cold milk, corn flour, cocoa powder and sugar. Cook this mixture on very low heat and stir constantly until it thickens. Do not boil. When the mixture, is sufficiently thick, top with the beaten egg whites and cook for 2 more minutes on low heat. Cool and serve

14. VANILLA BLANCMANGE

Serves 6   Time required: 1 hour

Ingredients
1 litre milk
100 grams sugar
2 teaspoons vanilla essence
50 grams corn flour

Mix the corn flour with ½ cup of milk to a smooth paste. Boil the remaining milk with sugar. Mix in the corn flour paste and vanilla essence and cook till the mixture thickens, stirring all the time.

Pour out into a dampened jelly mould and leave to set in a refrigerator. Remove from the fridge and dip the bottom of the mould in hot water, then turn out on a plate. Serve plain or with fresh fruit or jelly.

15. STRAWBERRY BLANCMANGE

Serves 6   Time required: 1 hour

Ingredients
1 cup sugar
3 tablespoons corn flour
¼ teaspoon salt
1 litre milk
2 teaspoons vanilla essence
1 cup fresh strawberries pureed

Mix the corn flour and salt in a little water. Boil the milk and sugar. When boiling, mix in the corn flour paste and vanilla essence. Cook till the mixture thickens, stirring all the time. Add the strawberry puree and mix well. Simmer for a few more minutes. Pour into dampened jelly moulds and set in a refrigerator. When set, remove from the refrigerator, then dip the bottom of the mould in hot water and turn out on a plate. Top with fresh cut strawberries and cream and serve

16. FRESH FRUIT TRIFLE

Serves 6   Time required: 1 hour

Ingredients
500 grams sponge cake
2 cups of fresh fruit such as banana, mango, apple, etc, peeled and chopped into small pieces
2 cups apple juice or mango juice
8 cherries chopped
Some chopped nuts for garnishing
200 grams fresh cream
4 tablespoons jam

Cut the cake into slices and lay them as the bottom layer in a flat glass dish. Mix the jam with the apple / mango juice and pour half the quantity all over the layer of cake. Next spread a layer of fruit over this using half the quantity of fruit, then spread a layer of fresh cream. Repeat the three layers again. Smoothen out the top layer of cream using a spatula. Garnish with chopped cherries and nuts. Chill and serve when required

17. TRIFLE SPONGE PUDDING

Serves 6   Time required: 1 hour

Ingredients
A square 500 grams sponge cake
1 can mixed fruits divided into 3 portions
4 tablespoons sugar
200 grams fresh cream divided into 3 portions
2 tablespoons jam
1 cup of mixed fresh fruit (optional)
100 grams cherries

Whip the fresh cream to soft peaks consistency. Slice the cake horizontally into 2 layers. Using a sharp knife, cut the cake to fit the bowl in which the pudding is to be set. Drain the excess syrup from the canned fruits. Make sugar syrup, using one cup of the excess canned fruit syrup. Add 2 tablespoons of the syrup to the jam and blend to a paste. Sprinkle the sugar syrup on the cake strips and divide them into 3 parts. Place a layer of cake in the glass bowl. Next arrange a layer of one portion of canned fruit over this and top it with a layer of one portion of fresh cream. Repeat as before with the remaining cake, fruit and cream. Smoothen out the top layer of cream using a spatula. Garnish with cherries and fresh fruit. Chill and serve when required.

18. TIPSY TRIFLE PUDDING

Serves 6   Time required: 1 hour

Ingredients
300 grams sponge cake
4 tablespoons mixed fruit jam
1 cup brandy or wine or sherry
1 large tin of canned mixed fruit divide into 3 portions
1 cup prepared jelly
100 grams candied cherries and walnuts (for decoration)
½ litre fresh cream

Whip the fresh cream to soft peaks consistency and divide into 3 parts. Drain the excess syrup from the canned fruits. Mix 2 tablespoons of jam to this fruit syrup and mix well. Add the brandy or sherry or wine to this syrup and divide into 3 portions. Divide the canned fruit into 3 parts. Using a sharp knife, slice the cake horizontally into 3 layers. So that they can fit the bottom of the bowl in which the pudding is to be set. (The layers may break but don't worry). Spread the 3 layers of cake liberally with jam. Place one of the cake layers in the glass bowl and soak with one portion of the whiskey and fruit syrup Press down firmly down. Now spread a layer of the tinned fruit over the soaked sponge cake layer. Top this layer with one portion of the fresh Cream.
Repeat the layers twice more as before with the remaining sponge cake, fruit and cream. Smoothen out the top layer of cream using a spatula. Garnish with cherries, walnuts (and fresh fruit). Chill and serve when required.

19. SIMPLE MILK PUDDING

Serves 6 Preparation time 1 hour

Ingredients
1 litre full cream milk.
1 can sweet condensed milk
1 teaspoon corn flour
4 slices white bread

1 teaspoon vanilla or almond essence
A few chopped nuts or cherries to garnish

Remove the crusts from the Bread and then cut each slice into one inch cubes. Mix the corn flour in ½ cup of cold milk till smooth. Keep aside. Boil the milk and condensed milk together till the quantity reduces. Mix in the corn flour and milk mixture and the vanilla or almond essence and mix well. Simmer on low heat, stirring all the time till the mixture thickens. Mix in the bread cubes and remove from heat.
Leave in the refrigerator to chill for a few hours before serving. Garnish with chopped nuts or cherries.

20. ROLY-POLY PUDDING

Serves 6   Time required: 1 hour

Ingredients
200 grams refined flour or maida
200 grams butter
100 grams sugar
A pinch of salt
2 eggs beaten well
1 teaspoon baking powder
4 tablespoons mixed fruit or strawberry jam
1 cup fresh cream whipped with 2 teaspoons sugar

Beat the butter and sugar together till fluffy. Add the eggs and continue beating for a few minutes. Add the flour, jam, salt and baking powder and mix well. Pour the mixture in a greased baking dish. Bake for 25 minutes until brown on the top. Remove from the oven and when cold turn over on a serving dish. Decorate with jam and whipped cream

21. BREAD PUDDING

Serves 6   Time required: 1 hour

Ingredients
3 cups Milk
8 slices of bread cut into cubes
200 grams butter
200 grams sugar
2 beaten eggs
1/4 tsp salt
200 grams raisins and chopped nuts
1 tsp vanilla essence

Arrange the bread in an oven proof glass dish. Boil the milk and set aside to cool for some time. When the milk is just warm, add all the other ingredients to it and mix well. (Except the chopped nuts and raisins) Pour over the bread cubes Sprinkle the chopped nuts and raisins on top. Bake at 180 degrees C for 40-45 minutes or until knife comes out clean. Serve warm with Ice Cream or Vanilla Sauce. The same pudding can be steamed in a pressure cooker as well.

22. BREAD AND BUTTER PUDDING

Serves 6   Time required: 1 hour

Ingredients
8 slices of bread
2 cups milk
50 grams butter
3 tablespoons sugar
1 teaspoon vanilla essence
½ cup chopped cashew nuts or walnuts
3 tablespoons raisins
2 tablespoons jam
2 eggs beaten well

Remove the crusts from the bread slices and butter them on both sides. Place 4 of the buttered slices in a greased baking dish. Sprinkle the raisins and nuts over them. Spread the jam on the remaining 4 buttered slices of bread and lay them (Jam side down) over the raisins and nuts. Mix the milk, beaten eggs, sugar and vanilla essence together and pour this mixture over the pieces of bread soaking them completely. Sprinkle some more raisins and nuts on the top. Bake in a moderate oven (180 Degrees C) for 20 to 30 minutes.

Note: This pudding can also be steamed for 30 minutes instead of baking if desired

23. RICE AND RAISIN PUDDING

Serves 6   Time required: 1 hour

Ingredients
100 grams Basmati rice or any other long grained rice washed and drained
3 tablespoons unsalted butter or ghee
1 litre milk
2 small pieces cinnamon
4 cloves
3 tablespoons soft brown sugar
100 grams raisins
1 teaspoon vanilla essence

Heat milk in a pan and bring to boil. Remove from heat then drop in the cinnamon and cloves. Mix in the brown sugar. Add the rice, raisins, vanilla essence and butter / ghee and mix well. Transfer to a suitable dish and dot the top with a little butter. Steam the pudding for 15 to 20 minutes. Serve with Ice cream.

24. BOMBAY PUDDING

Serves 6   Time required: 1 hour

Ingredients
8 slices bread
1 litre milk boiled and cooled
3 tablespoons sugar
½ teaspoon vanilla essence
1 tablespoon corn flour
2 eggs beaten
3 tablespoons jam

Beat the sugar, corn flour, vanilla essence and eggs together. Add the milk and mix well. Break the bread into small pieces and add to the milk mixture. Mix well.
Heat 1 tablespoon of sugar in a pudding mould till it melts and turns brown. Keep aside for 10 minutes to cool down.
Pour the bread mixture into the mould. Steam it for 30 minutes. Remove from the mould and spread jam on the top.
Cool and serve.

25. PINEAPPLE EMBASSY PUDDING

Serves 6   Time required: 1 hour

Ingredients
1 cup cream
1 teaspoon vanilla essence
½ cup sugar powdered
1 teaspoon gelatin
2 drops yellow food colour
¼ cup water
1 cup chopped pineapple
4 tablespoons chopped raisins and nuts

Whip the cream with the sugar, vanilla essence and yellow food colour.
Soak the gelatin in ¼ cup of water then dissolve it over low heat till

it melts completely. Cool, then add to the cream mixture. Mix in the chopped pineapple, raisins and nuts. Pour into a suitable glass dish or mould and leave in the refrigerator to set.

26. VICEROY'S BANANA PUDDING

Serves 6   Time required: 1 hour

Ingredients
200 grams refined flour or maida
200 grams butter
100 grams sugar
A pinch of salt
2 eggs beaten well
1 teaspoon baking powder
3 bananas cut into long slices
6 teaspoons lemon juice
1 cup fresh cream whipped with 2 teaspoons sugar
½ cup desiccated coconut

Beat the butter and sugar together till fluffy. Add the eggs and continue beating for a few minutes. Add in the flour, salt and baking powder and mix well. Pour the mixture in a greased baking dish. Arrange the banana slices evenly on top. Sprinkle lemon juice and desiccated coconut over the slices. Bake for 25 minutes (180 degrees C) until brown on the top. Remove from the oven and when cold turn over on a serving dish. Decorate with whipped cream.

27. ROSE MILK PUDDING

Serves 6 Preparation time 1 hour

Ingredients
1 tin condensed milk
1 litre full cream milk
25 grams china grass or gelatin
1 tablespoon rose essence

Mix condensed milk and milk together and boil. Soak china grass / gelatin in one cup of water for 10 minutes, then heat on low flame till it melts completely. Add the milk mixture and rose essence and simmer on low heat till the mixture thickens, stirring all the time. Pour into a suitable mould or dish and refrigerate till set. Serve plain or with fresh fruit.

28. NUTTY MOSS PUDDING

Serves 6 Preparation time 1 hour

Ingredients
1 tin condensed milk
1 litre full cream milk
25 grams china grass
1 tablespoon vanilla essence
3 tablespoons sugar
4 tablespoons chopped nuts

Soak china grass in one cup of water for 10 minutes. Mix condensed milk and milk together and boil. Heat the soaked china grass on low flame till it melts completely. Add the milk mixture, sugar, 3 tablespoons chopped nuts and vanilla essence and simmer on low heat till the mixture thickens, stirring all the time. Pour into a suitable mould or dish and sprinkle remaining nuts on top. Refrigerate till set.

29. CUSTARD CAKE

You'll enjoy the thrill of eating both a cake and custard

Serves 6   Time required: 1 hour
Ingredients for the Custard
6 eggs
1 cup of sweetened condensed milk
1 cup of skim milk
¼ cup of white sugar
½ teaspoon vanilla essence

Ingredients for the Cake
3 eggs (separate the yolks and whites in different bowls
½ cup of white sugar
¾ cup of cake flour
½ teaspoon of baking powder
1 teaspoon vanilla essence
¼ cup of skim milk

In a bowl beat ¼ cup of sugar, vanilla essence and egg yolks until smooth. In another bowl, beat the egg whites until foamy. Add the remaining ¼ cup of sugar little by little while beating continuously. Continue beating until the egg white mixture is stiff. Now you mix the egg yolk and egg white mixtures together.

Sift together the cake flour and baking powder. Now add the flour mixture and milk alternately, to the beaten eggs and sugar, mixing after each addition. After all the flour and milk have been added, mix until the batter is smooth by cutting and folding until the mixture is well blended and the color is even.

Pour the half the cake batter in a baking pan. Using a spatula, smoothen the top of the batter carefully.

Place all the ingredients for the custard in a bowl. Mix until the sugar is completely dissolved. The custard mixture should be of a little thick consistency. Do not beat as you do not want air bubbles in the mixture. Now pour the custard mixture over the layer of cake batter in the baking pan.

Pour the remaining cake batter over the custard. Smoothen the top carefully. Make sure that all the sides are sealed with the cake batter so that the custard does not boil over during baking. Sprinkle lots of granulated sugar on top.

Bake in a preheated 350oF oven for 50 minutes to an hour. After 50 minutes, insert a toothpick at the center of the cake. If it comes out clean, the cake is done. If not, bake a few minutes longer, testing every five minutes or so till the top is nicely browned.

Serve only when cold.

30. JELEBI CARAMEL CUSTARD

This is an old Colonial Dessert which was very famous during the days of the British raj. An Indian sweetmeat Jelabi is given a western touch with the addition of custard

Serves 6 Preparation time 1 hour

Ingredients
6 Jelebis (available in any Indian Sweet stall)
3 eggs beaten
½ tsp vanilla essence
½ litre milk
6 tablespoons sugar
A pinch of salt
4 tablespoons flour
1 teaspoon butter

Take a flat bottomed baking dish and grease it well with butter. Boil the milk and keep aside. Pre heat the oven till slightly warm. When the milk is slightly cold add the eggs, vanilla essence, flour and sugar and beat well till there are no lumps. Pour a thin layer of this mixture into the baking dish and let it set in the warm oven till it forms a base. Take out the dish and arrange the Jelebis in it. Pour the rest of the mixture over the Jelebis and bake for about 15 to 20 minutes till the custard sets and is golden brown on top. The custard should be moist and not dry. Garnish with sliced pistachios.

31. STRAWBERRY FLUMMERY

'Flummery' is a starch-based sweet soft dessert pudding known to have been popular in Britain and Ireland from the seventeenth to nineteenth centuries' It is usually topped with slices of fresh fruit and powdered sugar

Serves 6 Preparation time 1 hour

Ingredients
3 cups milk
1/4 cup cornstarch

5 tablespoons sugar
1 egg beaten
2 teaspoons vanilla extract
1 cup fresh sliced strawberries

Blend cornstarch with a little of the milk, stir into a sauce pan containing the rest of the milk and sugar. Bring to a boil and continue cooking over medium heat until mixture becomes thick. (Stir constantly). Stir in the beaten egg and continue cooking for 2 or 3 minutes more. Remove pan from heat and add vanilla extract. Pour into a glass serving bowl. Cover tightly and refrigerate for several hours. Arrange sliced strawberries berries evenly over top of pudding just before serving.

32. APPLE GRUNT

In olden days this pudding was cooked in a Dutch oven hanging over an open fire. The name "Grunt" presumably came from the sound the pudding made as it bubbled and grunted beneath the biscuit like topping.

Serves 6 Preparation time 1 hour

Ingredients
4 tablespoons butter
3 tablespoons brown sugar
2 cups pared cored and sliced fresh apples
2 tablespoons chopped walnuts
1 egg beaten
½ cup sugar
½ cup milk
1 teaspoon baking powder
1 cup all-purpose flour
½ liter whipped cream or ice cream

Sift the flour and baking powder together. Make a smooth batter with the flour, butter, egg and milk. Mix in the chopped walnuts. Take a non stick saucepan and melt the brown sugar slightly over low heat. Arrange the sliced apples over the brown sugar. Pour the batter over the apples. Just cover the saucepan tightly and simmer over low heat for 1 hour or till the cake is done. (You could bake in a moderate oven for 1 hour if desired)

Loosen cake from sides of pan with spatula and invert onto a serving platter. Serve with whipped cream or ice cream

Other fresh fruit such as mangoes, apples, pineapple, etc could be used instead of strawberries

----

IX

THE ANGLO-INDIAN SNACK BOX

THE ANGLO-INDIAN SNACK BOX is a collection of simple and easy to follow recipes of tasty snacks, short eats, nibbles and finger food that were regularly prepared in Anglo-Indian Homes and also at 'Parties, Soirees and Elegant Evening Gatherings' in the olden days - all innovated and made famous by the Mog Cooks of yore in the Tea Gardens in the Hills.

The repertoire covers a variety of vegetarian as well as non-vegetarian finger food and nibbles which include savouries, snacks, tea time treats, etc., that can easily be prepared from ingredients commonly available at home.

The recipes could be adapted to suit one's preferences. The Puffs, Patties, Cutlets and Rolls could be baked in an oven instead of frying if desired.

A. NIBBLES, FINGER FOOD, SMALL BITES, SAVOURIES & TEA TIME TREATS

1. CHICKEN SAUSAGE BITES

Serves 6   Time required: 45 minutes

Ingredients
5 or 6 Chicken Sausages
2 medium size onions sliced finely
2 teaspoons ground pepper or cracked pepper
1 tablespoon chopped garlic
Salt to taste
2 tablespoons oil

Boil the sausages in a little water then cut them into bite size pieces.
Heat oil in a pan and fry the finely chopped onions and chopped garlic
till the onions turn golden brown. Add the sausage pieces, pepper and
salt and mix well. Simmer on low flame for about 4 to 5 minutes, stirring
occasionally) till the sausage pieces take on the pepper and garlic flavor.
Serve as a starter or appetizer

Note: If desired, you could add pieces of capsicum also while frying the
onions and garlic to give it a different flavor.

2. CHICKEN AND CAPSICUM ON TOAST

Serves 6   Time required: 45 minutes

Ingredients
1 cup boiled and shredded chicken
1 onion chopped finely
1 capsicum chopped finely
1 cup chopped cucumber pieces
6 slices bread
1 teaspoon ground black pepper / pepper powder

3 tablespoons mayonnaise
Salt to taste

In a bowl mix all the ingredients except the bread together. Toast the bread till crisp. Cut each slice into quarters. Spoon the capsicum and chicken mixture on each piece. Serve with chillie garlic sauce.

3. LIVER ON TOAST

Serves 6   Time required: 45 minutes

Ingredients
½ kg liver either (beef, lamb or chicken) cut into small pieces
2 large onions sliced finely
2 teaspoons pepper powder / cracked pepper
Salt to taste
2 tablespoons oil
½ teaspoon turmeric powder

Boil the liver pieces with a little water and salt till soft.
Heat oil in a pan and fry the onions till golden brown. Add the cooked liver together with the turmeric powder, pepper powder and salt and keep frying on low heat till dry and brown.

Toast the bread till crisp. Cut each slice into quarters. Spoon the cooked liver mixture on each piece. Garnish each square with a single mint leaf. Serve hot

4. HAM AND CHEESE ON TOAST

Serves 6   Time required: 45 minutes

Ingredients
4 slices white or whole meal bread
3 teaspoons butter
1 tablespoon English mustard or Dijon mustard
½ teaspoon ground black pepper / black pepper powder

4 thick slices of ham
1 tablespoon finely chopped onions
3 tablespoons grated cheese
4 cherry tomatoes cut into quarters

Chop the ham into tiny bits and mix together with the butter, mustard, pepper and chopped onions. Toast the bread till crisp. Cut each slice into quarters. Spoon the ham and butter mixture on each piece. Garnish each square with the grated cheese and a piece of cherry tomato.

5. BEEF MINCE ON TOAST

Serves 6   Time required: 45 minutes

Ingredients
½ kg Mince (Beef or Mutton)
2 big Onions chopped
½ teaspoon turmeric powder
1 teaspoon chopped garlic
2 tablespoons oil
Salt to taste
2 teaspoons ground black pepper / pepper powder
4 slices bread either white or brown
A few coriander leaves to garnish

Heat oil in a pan and fry the chopped garlic and onions till golden brown.. Add the mince, turmeric powder, pepper powder and salt and mix well. Cook on low heat for about ½ an hour till the mince is cooked and nicely browned and dry. . Remove from heat.

Toast the bread till crisp. Cut each slice into quarters. Spoon the cooked mince mixture on each piece. Garnish each square with just a few chopped coriander leaves

6. BAKED BEANS ON TOAST

Serves 6   Time required: 45 minutes

Ingredients
4 slices brown bread or white bread
1 small can of baked beans
3 teaspoons butter
A few coriander leaves to garnish

Toast the bread till crisp then butter them on one side only. Cut each slice into quarters. Spoon the baked beans on each piece. Garnish each square with just a few chopped coriander leaves

7. CHICKEN FRITTERS

Serves 6   Time required: 45 minutes

Ingredients
½ kg boneless chicken cut into small pieces
3 tablespoons chillie garlic sauce
3 tablespoons corn flour
3 tablespoons plain flour (maida)
salt to taste
Oil for deep frying

Make a batter with the corn flour, plain flour / maida and salt with sufficient water. The batter should be slightly thick. Mix the chicken pieces with the sauce and mix into the batter. Heat oil in a pan and drop in spoonfuls of the mixture a little at a time and deep fry till golden brown. Use kitchen absorbent paper to remove excess oil. Serve hot with tomato sauce.

8. COCKTAIL CHICKEN CUTLETS

Serves 6   Time required: 45 minutes

Ingredients
½ kg chicken mince
2 tablespoons tomato sauce / ketchup
1 tablespoon lemon / lime juice
2 tablespoon chillie garlic sauce
1 teaspoon ground black pepper / pepper powder
Salt to taste
4 tablespoons plain flour / maida
3 tablespoons corn flour
oil for frying
½ cup milk
1 Egg Beaten
4 tablespoons bread crumbs

Cook the chicken mince, tomato ketchup / sauce, lemon / lime juice, chillie garlic sauce, pepper powder and a little salt till the mince is cooked and dry.
Make a thick batter with the flour / maida, corn flour, salt and milk. Form the chicken mince into small cutlets. Dip the cutlets one by one in the batter and roll in the bread crumbs.
Heat the oil in a pan and shallow fry the cocktail chicken cutlets till golden brown and crispy on both sides. Serve with chillie sauce.

Note: The chicken cutlets could be baked in the oven instead of frying if desired

9. CHICKEN BREAD ROLLS

Serves 6   Time required: 45 minutes

Ingredients
1 cup boiled and shredded chicken
2 tablespoons mayonnaise
1 teaspoon ground black pepper / pepper powder

Salt to taste
2 teaspoons chopped coriander leaves
2 green chillies chopped
2 onions finely chopped
12 slices bread

Mix the shredded chicken, mayonnaise, green chillies, coriander leaves, pepper powder, salt and onions in a bowl. Cut away the crusts from the bread. Flatten each slice with a rolling pin. Spread the filling on each slice and roll tightly. Tie each roll with a piece of thread. Heat oil in a deep pan and drop in the rolls slowly about 2 at a time. Reduce the heat and fry on medium heat till the rolls are light brown and crispy. Drain on a paper towel. Serve with tomato sauce.

Note: The chicken rolls could be baked in the oven instead of frying if desired

10. CHICKEN PUFFS

Serves 6   Time required: 45 minutes

Ingredients
3 cups refined flour / maida
½ kg boneless chicken chopped into small pieces
2 onions chopped
Salt to taste
1 teaspoon chillie powder
2 teaspoons chopped coriander leaves
1 teaspoon chopped ginger
1 teaspoon chopped garlic
½ teaspoon cumin powder
50 grams butter
½ teaspoon baking powder
Sufficient Oil for frying

Sift the flour with a teaspoon of salt and baking powder. Mix the butter with the flour and knead into a stiff dough using very little water. Keep aside.

Heat 2 tablespoons oil in a pan and sauté the chopped ginger, garlic and onions lightly. Add the boneless chicken chillie powder, cumin powder, coriander leaves and salt. Stir well and cook on low heat till the chicken is cooked and all the water dries up. Remove and keep aside to cool.

Now take the prepared pastry dough onto a floured board and rollout into a thin sheet. Cut rounds of about 10 cm diameter with a saucer. Spoon a little of the chicken mixture on one half of the rounds and fold the other half over. Seal the edges by dampening with a little water. Prepare the puffs in this way till all the dough and mince is used up.

Heat the oil for frying in a fairly deep pan till smoky. Slowly drop in the puffs one by one (as many as the pan can hold). Fry till crisp and brown on both sides. Remove from the oil and drain. Serve hot

Note: The chicken puffs could be baked in the oven instead of frying if desired

11. CHICKEN PATTIES

Serves 6   Time required: I hour

Ingredients
1 kg chicken mince
1 cup breadcrumbs
2 eggs beaten
3 onions chopped finely
1 tablespoon chopped coriander leaves
Salt to taste
1 teaspoon ground black pepper / pepper powder
½ teaspoon spice powder (garam masala powder)
6 tablespoons oil

Heat 2 tablespoon oil in a pan and sauté the onions lightly. Add the chicken mince and a little salt and cook till the chicken is cooked. Remove from heat then mix the chicken with the breadcrumbs, chopped coriander leaves, beaten eggs, salt, pepper and spice powder. Mix well then form into small round patties. Heat the remaining oil in a flat pan and fry the patties on medium heat till golden brown on both sides

Note: The Chicken Patties could be baked in the oven instead of frying if desired

12. CHICKEN ROLLS

Serves 6   Time required: 1 hour

Ingredients
500 grams boneless chicken
2 capsicums cut into ½ inch pieces
1 teaspoon cumin powder
1 teaspoon chopped garlic
2 tablespoons vinegar
1 teaspoon chillie powder
1 teaspoon ground black pepper / pepper powder
Salt to taste
2 green chillies chopped
1 onion chopped finely
1 tablespoon chopped coriander leaves
6 Soft Chapattis
2 tablespoons oil

Marinate the chicken with the chillie powder, pepper powder, cumin powder, garlic, vinegar and salt and leave aside for an hour.

Heat oil in a pan and add the marinated chicken. Simmer on low heat till the chicken is cooked and all the water dries up. Toss in the capsicum and mix well. Cook for 5 minutes till the capsicum is half cooked. Remove from heat.

Place a few teaspoons of the cooked chicken on the chapattis lengthwise. Sprinkle some chopped onions, green chillies and coriander leaves on top then form into a roll. Wrap the bottom of the roll in a paper napkin or some foil and serve with chillie sauce and tomato ketchup. The Rolls could be cut into two and served if desired.

13. FRIED CHICKEN DRUMSTICKS

Serves 6   Time required: 1 hour

Ingredients
8 Chicken Drumsticks
2 tablespoons corn flour
1 egg beaten
½ teaspoon baking powder
3 tablespoons refined flour / maida
2 tablespoons soya sauce
salt to taste
2 teaspoons ground black pepper / pepper powder
1 teaspoon cumin powder
Oil for frying

Marinate the chicken drumsticks with all the above ingredients (except oil) for about 2 hours. Heat oil in a pan and deep fry the chicken drumsticks 2 at a time till golden brown. Serve with chillie sauce. *Note: The Chicken Patties could be baked in the oven instead of frying if desired*

14. CRUMB FRIED CHICKEN

Serves 6   Time required: 1 hour

Ingredients
6 chicken breasts (flattened)
2 teaspoons ground black pepper / pepper powder
Salt to taste
1 teaspoon garlic paste
2 teaspoons refined flour
2 eggs beaten
4 tablespoons bread crumbs
4 tablespoons oil

Mix the flour, egg, garlic, pepper powder and salt together. Marinate the chicken breasts with this mixture. Heat oil in a flat pan. Roll each chicken breast in the bread crumbs and shallow fry on low heat till golden brown.

15. FRIED CHICKEN CHUNKS

Serves 6   Time required: 1 hour

Ingredients
1kg boneless chicken
2 teaspoons ginger garlic paste
2 tablespoons red chillie powder
2 teaspoons cumin powder
2 tablespoons vinegar
¼ teaspoon orange food colour (Optional)
Salt to taste
2 teaspoons thick yogurt / curds
Oil for frying

Mix the ginger garlic paste, chillie powder, cumin powder, vinegar, yogurt, orange food colour and salt together in a small bowl and then marinate the boneless chicken pieces with this mixture for about one hour.

Heat the oil in a pan, and fry the marinated chicken chunks a few at a time, till golden brown. Pierce each chunk with a tooth- pick and serve with lemon slices and Onion Rings

Note: The chicken could be grilled in the oven instead of frying if desired.

16. FRIED PEPPER CHICKEN

Serves 6   Time required: 1 hour

Ingredients
500 grams boneless chicken cut into one-inch size pieces
3 teaspoons ground black pepper / black pepper powder
2 teaspoons ginger garlic paste
1 egg beaten
Salt to taste
2 teaspoons lemon juice
Oil for frying

Marinate the chicken with the pepper powder, ginger garlic paste, egg, salt and lemon juice and set aside for 1 hour. Heat oil in a pan and deep fry the chicken pieces till crisp.
Serve hot with Onion Rings and mint chutney
Note: The Chicken could be grilled in the oven instead of frying if desired

17. BLACK PEPPER CHICKEN WINGS

Serves 6   Time required: 1 hour

Ingredients
12 chicken wings
1 teaspoon ginger garlic paste
3 tablespoons corn flour
2 teaspoons ground black pepper / pepper powder
2 teaspoons soya sauce or Worcestershire sauce
Salt to taste

Marinate the chicken wings with all the above ingredients. Heat sufficient oil in a pan and deep fry the chicken wings two at a time till crisp and golden brown. Serve with chillie sauce
Note: The Chicken wings could be grilled in the oven instead of frying if desired

18. SPICY CHICKEN WINGS

Serves 6   Time required: 1 hour

Ingredients
20 medium sized chicken wings
2 teaspoons chillie powder
1 teaspoons ground black pepper / black pepper powder
1 teaspoon ginger garlic paste
2 eggs beaten
3 teaspoons corn flour
Salt to taste
2 teaspoons lemon juice
Oil for frying

Cut the tips of the chicken wings then marinate them with all the above ingredients except the oil and set aside for 1 hour. Heat oil in a pan and deep fry the chicken wings till crisp. Serve hot with Onion Rings and mint chutney

19. MUTTON / LAMB CROQUETTES / RISSOLES

Serves 6   Time required: 1 hour

Ingredients
300 grams boneless mutton or lamb chopped into small pieces
3 onions chopped
2 teaspoons chopped mint
1 teaspoon ground black pepper / pepper powder
Salt to taste
2 tablespoons tomato sauce
1 teaspoon butter
1 egg beaten
Yolk of one egg
3 tablespoons oil
3 tablespoons bread crumbs

Cook the mutton or lamb pieces in a little water with some salt and turmeric till tender and all the soup dries up. Remove from the heat and set aside to cool.

Shred the meat into very small flakes. Mix in the chopped onions, mint, pepper, salt, sauce, butter and the egg yolk. Form into cigar shaped croquettes.

Heat the oil in a flat pan. Dip each croquette in the beaten Egg, roll in bread crumbs then shallow fry on both sides till brown. Drain and serve with mashed potatoes.

Note: Minced Meat can also be used instead. Cook the mince with a little water then proceed as above to make the croquettes. Cold leftover roast meat can also be made into croquettes

20. MUTTON /LAMB / BEEF MINCE ROLLS

Serves 6   Time required: 1 hour

Ingredients
½ kg mutton / lamb mince
2 big onions chopped
½ teaspoon turmeric powder
1 teaspoon chopped garlic
1teaspoon chopped ginger
3 green chilies chopped finely
2 tablespoons chopped coriander leaves
2 tablespoons oil
Salt to taste
½ teaspoon chillie powder
6 soft chapattis

Heat the oil in a pan and fry the onions till golden brown. Add the mince, salt, chopped ginger, garlic, green chilies, turmeric powder, chillie powder and sauté for 3 minutes. Add the chopped coriander leaves and cook on low heat till the mince is cooked and all the water evaporates and the mince is quite dry.
Place a few teaspoons of the cooked mince on the chapattis lengthwise. Sprinkle some chopped onions, green chillies and coriander leaves on top then form into a roll. Wrap the bottom of the roll in a paper napkin or foil and serve with chillie sauce and tomato ketchup

21. MUTTON / BEEF MINCE PATTIES

Serves 6   Time required: 1 hour

Ingredients
½ kg fine mutton, lamb or beef mince
½ teaspoon chopped ginger
½ teaspoon chopped garlic
1 medium sized onion chopped finely
2 green chilies chopped finely
1 teaspoon ground black pepper / pepper powder

Salt to taste
1 tablespoon chopped mint
3 tablespoons oil
1 egg beaten
2 tablespoons breadcrumbs
3 large potatoes

Boil the potatoes, remove the skin and mash well. Keep aside.

In a pan add the mince, ginger, garlic, onions, green chilies, pepper powder and salt with a little oil and cook till the mince is dry. Remove from heat and cool for some time. Mix it well with the potatoes.

Form into oval or round shapes, flatten and dip in the beaten egg then roll in the breadcrumbs.

Heat the oil in a flat pan and shallow fry the patties on low heat till golden brown on both sides. Serve with tomato sauce or mint chutney

22. MUTTON / LAMB / BEEF CUTLETS

Serves 6   Time required: 1 hour

Ingredients
½ kg minced mutton / Lamb or Beef
1 large onion chopped
1 teaspoon ginger garlic paste
3 green chillies chopped
2 slices of bread
4 tablespoons dry bread crumbs
2 eggs beaten
Salt to taste
1 teaspoon ground black pepper / pepper powder
1 teaspoon chillie powder
1 teaspoon cumin powder
1 tablespoon chopped coriander leaves
Oil for frying

Cook the minced meat, chopped onion, green chillies, ginger paste, garlic paste, chillie powder, cumin powder, salt and pepper powder till tender and dry. Soak the slices of bread in water and squeeze. Mix it into the cooked minced meat together with the chopped coriander leaves, 2 tablespoons bread crumbs and 1 beaten egg.

Heat the oil in a shallow pan. Take small balls of the mixture and form into oval shaped cutlets. Dip each one into the remaining beaten egg, coat with the bread crumbs and shallow fry till golden brown. Serve hot with tomato sauce and salad.

23. COCKTAIL MUTTON / LAMB / BEEF CUTLETS

Serves 6   Time required: 1 hour

Ingredients
300 grams mutton /lamb or Beef mince
3 slices of bread
1 large onion
2 teaspoons ginger garlic paste
2 teaspoons cumin powder
3 teaspoons chopped coriander leaves
2 eggs beaten
2 teaspoons red chillie powder
Salt to taste
3 tablespoons oil

Cook the mince meat together with the onion, ginger garlic paste, cumin powder, chillie powder and salt with very little water (on low heat) till tender and dry. Remove from heat and set aside to cool.

When cold, grind to a rough paste in a blender. Soak the slices of bread in water and squeeze dry. Mix the eggs and bread with the cooked mince. Form in to small round balls, and flatten them.

Heat oil in a shallow pan and fry the cocktail cutlets till golden brown. Insert a toothpick in each cutlet. Serve hot with a yogurt or curd Dip.

24. FISH CUTLETS

Serves 6   Time required: 1 hour

Ingredients
300 grams good fleshy fish fillets
2 teaspoons chopped mint
1 teaspoon ground black pepper / pepper powder
Salt to taste
2 tablespoons tomato sauce
1 teaspoon butter
1 egg beaten
Yolk of one egg
3 tablespoons oil
3 tablespoons bread crumbs
1 cup boiled and mashed potatoes

Wash the fish and cook in a little water with some salt for about 6 minutes or till the fish is cooked. Remove from the heat and cool. When cold mash the fish with a fork. Mix in the mashed potatoes, mint, pepper, salt, tomato sauce, butter and the egg yolk. Form into oval or round shapes and flatten with a knife.

Heat the oil in a flat pan. Dip each fish cutlet in the beaten egg, roll in bread crumbs then shallow fry on both sides till brown. Serve with any chutney, onion rings and tomato sauce.

Note: 1 tin of Tuna Fish can be used instead of the fresh fish to make Tuna Fish Cutlets

25. FISH FRITTERS

Serves 6   Time required: 1 hour

Ingredients
½ kg boneless fish cut into strips
3 tablespoons flour
Salt to taste

1 teaspoon chillie powder
Oil for frying

Wash the fish and leave to drain. Mix the flour, salt and chillie powder together with a little water to make a slightly thick batter. Coat each piece of fish well with the batter.
Heat oil in a pan till smoky and fry the coated fish pieces till brown on both sides. Drain and serve hot with tomato sauce.

26. FISH FINGERS

Serves 6   Time required: 1 hour

Ingredients
½ kg boneless fish cut into strips
2 eggs beaten well
3 tablespoons refined flour or maida
Salt to taste
1 teaspoon ground black pepper / pepper powder
1 teaspoon chillie powder
1 teaspoon cumin powder
½ kg oil for frying

Wash the fish and leave to dry. Mix the flour together with all the above ingredients (except the oil) with a little water to make a slightly thick batter. Coat each piece of fish well with the batter. Heat oil in a pan till smoky and fry the coated fish pieces till brown on both sides. Drain and serve hot with tomato sauce

27. FISH CROQUETTES / RISSOLES

Serves 6   Time required: 1 hour

Ingredients
500 grams fish fillets of any good fleshy fish
2 teaspoons cumin powder
1 teaspoon ginger garlic paste

1 large onion finely chopped
3 green chillies finely chopped
3 tablespoons bread crumbs
1 teaspoon ground black pepper / pepper powder
1 egg yolk
Salt to taste
3 tablespoons oil

Wash the fish and boil in a little salted water for 5 minutes. Drain away the excess soup and keep aside. Mash the fish coarsely.
Mix all the other ingredients (except the oil) with the mashed fish. Heat the oil in a shallow pan. Take small balls of the Fish mixture and form into cigar shaped cutlets. Dip each one into a beaten egg, coat with the bread crumbs and shallow fry till golden brown. Serve hot with tomato sauce and any other sauce.

28. CRISPY FRIED FISH NUGGETS

Serves 6   Time required: 1 hour

Ingredients
500 grams fleshy fish fillets cut into nuggets or cubes
1 teaspoon cumin powder
2 teaspoons chillie powder
1 teaspoon ginger paste
Salt to taste
2 teaspoons vinegar
3 tablespoons crushed corn flakes
Oil for frying

Wash the fish and marinate it with all the above ingredients (except the oil). Heat oil in a pan till smoky and fry the fish nuggets till golden brown on both sides. Squeeze lemon juice on the nuggets when done. Drain and serve hot with mint chutney and onion rings.

29. BATTER FRIED PRAWNS

Serves 6   Time required: 1 hour

Ingredients
½ kg medium size prawns
4 tablespoons flour
1 teaspoon chillie powder
Salt to taste
1 egg beaten
Oil as required for deep frying

Wash, clean and de-vein the pawns. Make a slightly thick batter with the flour, chillie powder, salt, beaten egg and a little water. Dip the prawns in the batter and deep fry till golden brown.

30. SPICY FRIED PRAWNS

Serves 6   Time required: 1 hour

Ingredients
½ kg big prawns
1 teaspoon ginger garlic paste
2 teaspoons red chillie powder
1 teaspoon all spice powder / garam masala
1 tablespoon vinegar
1 tablespoon lemon juice
2 tablespoons butter
Salt to taste
3 tablespoons oil

Clean, de-vein and wash the prawns well. Marinate the prawns with the ginger garlic paste, red chillie powder, all spice powder, vinegar, lemon juice, butter and salt and set it aside for one hour. Heat the oil in a pan till smoky and fry the Prawns till golden brown. Squeeze lemon juice on the prawns when done. Drain and serve hot with onion rings and lemon wedges.

31. GRILLED PRAWNS

Serves 6   Time required: 1 hour

Ingredients
1 kg good tiger prawns
2 teaspoons chillie powder
3 tablespoons curds or yogurt
Salt to taste
½ teaspoon turmeric powder
1 teaspoon coriander powder
1 teaspoon ginger garlic paste
2 teaspoons oil

Shell, de-vein and wash the prawns well. Marinate the prawns with all the above ingredients for about 45 minutes. Place the marinated prawns in a greased baking dish and grill in a hot oven for 10 to 15 minutes. (Alternately fry the prawns till golden brown) Serve with onion rings and chips.

32. EGG FRITTERS

Serves 6   Time required: 1 hour

Ingredients
4 hard boiled eggs cut into quarters
1 cup gram flour
1 onion chopped
2 green chilies chopped
1 teaspoon chopped coriander leaves
½ teaspoon salt
¼ teaspoon baking soda or baking powder
Oil for frying

Mix all the above ingredients together (except the oil) to form a sticky batter. Heat the oil in a deep frying pan till smoky. Drop in teaspoonfuls of batter with a piece of egg, into the hot oil and fry till golden brown. Remove and serve with tomato sauce or chutney.

33. SCOTCH EGGS

Scotch Eggs are traditionally prepared with Pork sausage mince. However, since many people don't eat pork, I've adapted the recipe so that either beef mince or Mutton Lamb Mince could be used instead of the Pork Mince.

Serves 6   Time required: 1 hour

Ingredients
500g Fine Beef or Mutton / Lamb Mince
2 teaspoons Worcestershire sauce
6 hard-boiled eggs, peeled
1 teaspoon ground black pepper / pepper powder
1 tablespoon plain flour
Salt to taste
1 egg, beaten
4 tablespoons dried breadcrumbs
Oil for deep frying

In a medium bowl, mix together the mince and Worcestershire sauce. Then mix in the flour, salt and pepper. Divide the mince mixture into 6 equal parts. Mold and encase each part around one of the hard-boiled eggs, rolling between your hands to shape. Place the beaten egg and breadcrumbs into separate dishes. Dip the encased eggs into the beaten egg, then roll in the breadcrumbs until coated. Deep fry the coated eggs until golden brown.
Serve with mustard sauce and green salad

34. EGG POTATO CHOPS

Serves 6   Time required: 1 hour

Ingredients
8 hard-boiled eggs cut into halves
3 potatoes boiled and mashed
2 slices bread
1 teaspoon ground black pepper / black pepper powder
Salt to taste

½ cup bread crumbs
1 egg beaten

Soak the bread in water, squeeze and crush. Mix it with the mashed potato, salt and pepper powder. Make even sized balls of the potato dough and place a half hardboiled egg in the centre of each potato ball. Cover the eggs well with the potato mixture and make them oval shaped. Dip each covered egg in the beaten Egg, roll in bread crumbs and deep fry in hot oil till golden brown. Serve hot with mint chutney or tomato ketch up

35. EGG CROQUETTES / RISSOLES

Serves 6   Time required: 1 hour

Ingredients
6 hardboiled eggs peeled and cut into quarters
3 large potatoes boiled and mashed
2 teaspoons cumin powder
1 large onion finely chopped
3 green chillies finely chopped
3 tablespoons bread crumbs
1 teaspoon ground black pepper / pepper powder
1 egg yolk
Salt to taste
3 tablespoons oil

Mix all the other ingredients together (except the oil) with the quartered boiled eggs.
Heat the oil in a shallow pan. Take small balls of the potato and egg mixture and form into cigar shaped croquettes / rissoles. Dip each one into a beaten egg, coat with the bread crumbs and shallow fry till golden brown. Serve hot with tomato sauce and any other sauce.

36. DEVILLED EGGS

Serves 6   Time required: 1 hour

Ingredients
6 hard-boiled eggs
2 tablespoons mayonnaise
2 teaspoons Dijon mustard
1 medium sized onion chopped finely
2 tablespoons finely chopped coriander leaves or parsley
1 teaspoon freshly ground black pepper
Salt, to taste
1 teaspoon Paprika (optional)

Slice the hard boiled eggs lengthwise. Scoop out the yolks with a teaspoon into a bowl and then mash well. Add the mayonnaise and Dijon Mustard and mash well until desired consistency is reached. Stir in the onion and most of the chopped coriander leaves / parsley. Add salt and pepper to taste. Using a small teaspoon or icing piping bag, fill the egg white halves with the yolk paste. Garnish with the remaining chopped coriander leaves / parsley. Sprinkle a little pepper and/or paprika, if desired. Serve on a bed of lettuce leaves with sliced tomatoes around the plate/

37. VEGETABLE PATTIES

Serves 6   Time required: 1 hour

Ingredients
1 cup of chopped boiled vegetables such as peas, carrots, French beans etc
3 potatoes boiled and mashed
2 onions chopped finely
2 green chillies chopped
1 teaspoon chopped mint
1 teaspoon finely chopped ginger
½ teaspoon ground black pepper / pepper powder
Salt to taste

3 tablespoons oil
1 egg beaten
3 tablespoons breadcrumbs

Heat oil in a pan and fry the onions and ginger till golden brown. Add the chopped green chillies and sauté for a minute. Now add the cooked vegetables, salt, and mint and mix well. Cook on low heat for about 5 minutes, then set aside to cool for some time. Now mix in the mashed potato and mint. Make even sized balls with the mixture and form into round cutlets.
Heat the oil in a flat pan. Dip each Patty in beaten egg, roll in powdered breadcrumbs and shallow fry till golden brown on both sides. Serve hot with tomato sauce or chutney.

38. VEGETABLE PUFFS

Serves 6   Time required: 1 hour

Ingredients
3 cups refined flour / maida
1 cup of chopped boiled vegetables such as peas, carrots, French beans, potato, etc
2 onions chopped
50 grams butter
½ teaspoon baking powder
1/2 kg oil for frying
Salt to taste
1teaspoon chillie powder
½ teaspoon cumin powder
2 teaspoons chopped coriander leaves
1 teaspoon chopped ginger

Sift the flour with a teaspoon of salt and baking powder. Mix the butter with the flour and knead into a stiff dough using very little water. Keep aside.

Heat 2 tablespoons oil in a pan and sauté the chopped ginger and onions lightly. Add all the vegetables, chillie powder, coriander leaves, cumin powder, and salt. Add a little water. Stir well and cook on low heat till the vegetables are cooked and all the water dries up. Remove and keep aside to cool.

Now take the prepared pastry dough onto a floured board and rollout into a thin sheet. Cut rounds of about 10 cm diameter with a saucer. Put a little of the cooked vegetable on one half of the rounds and fold the other half over. Seal the edges by dampening with a little water. Prepare the puffs in this way till all the dough and mince is used up.

Heat the oil for frying in a fairly deep pan till smoky. Slowly drop in the puffs one by one (as many as the pan can hold). Fry till crisp and brown on both sides. Remove from the oil and drain. Serve hot

39. MIXED VEGETABLE CROQUETTES / RISSOLES

Serves 6   Time required: 1 hour

Ingredients
2 cups of any mixed vegetables such as carrots, peas, beans, potatoes, etc.
1 teaspoon chopped garlic
1 teaspoon chopped ginger
2 teaspoons red chillie powder
1 teaspoon cumin powder
2 teaspoons lemon juice
2 teaspoons chopped coriander leaves
1 teaspoon chopped mint
1 egg beaten
2 tablespoons flour
3 slices of bread
Salt to taste
4 tablespoons oil or butter for frying

Cook the mixed vegetables with a little water and mash well. Mix in the chopped garlic, ginger, red chillie powder, cumin powder, coriander leaves, mint and salt. Remove from heat and keep aside.

Soak the bread in water then squeeze dry. Mix it with the mashed vegetables

Form small oval shaped croquettes or rissoles with the mixed vegetable mixture. Make a batter with the egg and flour.

Heat the oil in a shallow pan. Dip the croquettes in the flour and egg mixture and shallow fry the croquettes few at a time till golden brown. Serve hot as a snack with onion rings and tomato sauce

40. POTATO PATTIES

Serves 6   Time required: 1 hour

Ingredients
½ Kg potatoes boiled and mashed
2 slices bread
3 teaspoons chopped coriander leaves
2 green chillies chopped
½ teaspoon ground black pepper / pepper powder
3 tablespoons bread crumbs
½ teaspoon chopped ginger
Salt to taste
1 egg beaten

Soak the bread in water, squeeze and crush. Mix with the mashed potato and all the other ingredients (except the bread crumbs and beaten eggs). Make small balls of the potato dough. Flatten and shape into patties. Dip each in the beaten egg, roll in bread crumbs and shallow fry in hot oil on both sides till golden brown. Serve hot with mint chutney or tomato ketch up

41. POTATO CHOPS

Serves 6   Time required: 1 hour

Ingredients
½ Kg potatoes boiled and mashed
2 slices bread
3 teaspoons chopped coriander leaves

2 green chillies chopped
1 teaspoon ground black pepper / pepper powder
3 tablespoons bread crumbs
½ teaspoon chopped ginger
Salt to taste
1 egg beaten

Soak the bread in water, squeeze and crush. Mix with the mashed potato and all the other ingredients (except the bread crumbs and beaten eggs). Make small balls of the potato dough. Flatten and shape into patties. Dip each in the beaten egg, roll in bread crumbs and shallow fry in hot oil on both sides till golden brown. Serve hot with mint chutney or tomato ketch up.

42. SPICY POTATO WEDGES

Serves 6   Time required: 1 hour

Ingredients
3 large potatoes
I teaspoon red chillie powder
2 teaspoons corn flour
Salt to taste
Oil for deep frying

Cook the potatoes in sufficient water till just soft. Peel the skins and chop roughly into wedges. Mix in the chillie powder, corn flour and salt. Heat oil in a deep pan and when sufficiently hot, fry the potato wedges till golden brown. Serve as a starter with mint chutney or tomato sauce.

43. CRUMBED FRIED POTATO WEDGES

Serves 6   Time required: 1 hour

Ingredients
½ Kg potatoes boiled and cut into thick wedges
3 teaspoons chopped coriander leaves
1teaspoon chillie powder

½ teaspoon cumin powder
½ teaspoon ground black pepper / pepper powder
3 tablespoons bread crumbs
½ teaspoon chopped ginger
Salt to taste
1 egg beaten

Marinate the potato wedges with beaten egg, chillie powder, coriander leaves, cumin powder, pepper powder, chopped ginger and salt for half an hour. Roll each wedge in bread crumbs and shallow fry in hot oil on both sides till golden brown. Serve hot with mint chutney or tomato ketch up.

44. ONION AND SPINACH FRITTERS

Serves 6   Time required: 1 hour

Ingredients
1 cup Gram flour
1 onion chopped
3 tablespoons chopped spinach leaves
2 green chilies chopped
½ teaspoon salt
¼ teaspoon baking soda or baking powder
Oil for frying

Mix all the above ingredients together (except the oil) to form a sticky batter. Heat the oil in a deep frying pan till smoky. Drop in a teaspoonful of batter at a time into the hot oil and fry till golden brown. Remove and serve with tomato sauce or chutney.

45. CRISPY CAULIFLOWER FRITTERS

Serves 6   Time required: 1 hour

Ingredients
1 small cauliflower cut into florets
2 teaspoons chillie powder

Salt to taste
3 tablespoons cornflower
4 tablespoons refined flour / maida
Oil for frying

Soak the cauliflower florets in a bowl of water with a pinch of salt for ½ an hour. Wash and drain. Make a paste with the chillie powder, salt, corn flour and refined flour with a little water. Mix the cauliflower with this paste and set aside for 20 minutes. Heat oil in a pan and deep fry the cauliflower florets a few at a time till crispy and golden brown. Serve with chillie sauce and mint chutney

46. CHEESE STRAWS

Serves 6   Time required: 1 hour

Ingredients
500 grams plain flour
1 teaspoon salt
250 grams butter or margarine
5 tablespoons water
250 grams shredded cheddar cheese
½ teaspoon baking powder
Oil for frying

Sift the flour, salt and baking powder together. Empty into a bowl and add the butter, and cheese. Mix lightly. Now add the water a little at a time until the flour is moistened and forms a ball. (Add a little more water if required).
Turn the dough out onto a floured surface and roll out into a rectangle shape about ¼ inch thick. Cut the dough into 3 inch strips. Heat oil in a pan and deep fry the strips till golden brown. Drain and serve.

(Alternately, place these strips on an ungreased baking tray and bake at 200 degrees C for 10 minutes until the cheese straws are golden and puff up).

47. CHILLIE CHEESE STICKS

Serves 6   Time required: 1 hour

Ingredients
2 cupsplain flour
1 teaspoon salt
2 teaspoons chillie powder
1 teaspoon baking powder
200 grams butter or margarine
200 grams shredded cheddar cheese
½ teaspoon pepper powder
½ cup sour curds or yogurt
Oil for frying

Mix all the above ingredients together (except the oil) and chill for about 2 hours in a refrigerator. Take out and leave to attain room temperature. Roll out the dough into a rectangle shape about ¼ inch thick on a floured surface. Cut the dough into 3 inch strips about ¼ inch wide.
Heat sufficient oil in a pan and deep fry the strips till golden.

Alternately, place these strips on an ungreased baking tray and bake at 200 degrees C for 10 minutes until the cheese sticks are golden and puff up.

48. CHEESE TWISTS

Serves 6   Time required: 1 hour

Ingredients
2 cups plain flour / maida
1 teaspoon baking powder
½ teaspoon salt
1 teaspoon white pepper powder
2 tablespoons butter
½ cup shredded cheddar cheese
½ cup milk
Oil for frying

Sift flour, salt, baking powder, and pepper into a medium size mixing bowl. Mix in the butter or margarine and cheese and knead lightly until mixture is crumbly. Sprinkle cold water over mixture; and knead lightly until mixture holds together and leaves side of bowl.

Roll out on to a floured board to about ½ inch thick. Cut crosswise into strips about ½ inch wide. Lift the strips carefully and twist each one gently. Heat sufficient oil in a pan and deep fry the strips till golden.

Alternately, place these strips on an ungreased baking tray and bake at 200 degrees C for 10 minutes until the cheese Twists turn golden and puff up.

49. MINCE CURRY PUFFS

Serves 6   Time required: 1 hour 40 minutes

Ingredients for the Dough:
2 cups refined flour or maida
50 grams butter
½ teaspoon baking powder
1 teaspoon salt
Oil for frying.

For the Filling:
250 grams minced meat (Beef, Lamb or Mutton)
2 teaspoons chillie powder
2 medium size onions (chopped)
2 teaspoons chopped coriander leaves
Salt to taste
1 teaspoon ginger garlic paste

To prepare the pastry dough: Sift the flour with a teaspoon of salt and baking powder. Mix the butter with the flour and knead into a stiff dough using very little water. Keep aside.

To prepare the filling: Heat 1 tablespoon oil in a pan and sauté the onions lightly. Add the meat mince, chillie powder, ginger garlic paste, coriander leaves and salt. Stir well and cook on low heat till the mince is cooked and all the water dries up. Remove and keep aside to cool.

Now take the prepared pastry dough onto a floured board and rollout into a thin sheet. Cut rounds of about 10 cm diameter with a saucer. Put a little mince on one half of the rounds and fold the other half over. Seal the edges by dampening with a little water. Prepare the puffs in this way till all the dough and mince is used up.

Heat the oil for frying in a fairly deep pan till smoky. Slowly drop in the puffs one by one (as many as the pan can hold). Fry till crisp and brown on both sides. Remove from the oil and drain. Serve hot.

Note: Alternately, these puffs could be baked in an oven instead of frying them

50. SWEET COCONUT PUFFS

Serves 6   Time required: 1 hour 40 minutes

Ingredients

For the Dough:
2 cups refined flour or maida
50 grams butter
½ teaspoon baking powder
1 teaspoon salt
Oil for frying

For the Filling:
3 cups grated coconut and 2 tablespoons sugar mixed together

Sift the flour with the salt and baking powder. Mix in the butter and knead to a fairly stiff dough with very little water. Keep aside for 1 hour.

Take the dough on a floured board and roll out into a thin sheet. Cut squares of about 2 to 3 inches per side. Put a tablespoon of the sweetened coconut on half of the square. Fold the other half over in such a way to form a triangle. Seal the edges by dampening with a little water.

Heat the oil in a deep pan till smoky. Slowly drop in as many puffs as the pan can hold and fry till brown on both sides. Remove from the pan and drain.

Note: These puffs can last for a fortnight if dry cocoanut or copra is used instead of fresh coconut. Alternately, these puffs could be baked in an oven instead of frying them

51. MINCE PANTHRAS /FRIED MINCE PAN ROLLS

Serves 6   Time required: 1 hour 20 minutes

Ingredients for the Pan Rolls
2 cups flour
2 eggs beaten
1 cup milk
2 tablespoons melted butter
A pinch salt

Ingredients for the Mince
500 grams minced meat either beef, mutton or chicken
1 onion chopped finely
1 teaspoon chopped garlic
1 teaspoon chopped ginger
2 medium size potatoes peeled and cut into 2cm cubes
Salt to taste
2 teaspoons chillie powder
1 teaspoon garam masala powder or all spice powder
1 teaspoon cumin powder
1 teaspoon coriander powder
1 egg lightly beaten
Oil for deep frying
1 cup dry bread crumbs

Cook the mince along with the chopped onion, garlic, ginger, potatoes, chillie powder, garam masala / all spice powder, cumin powder, coriander powder and salt with half cup of water on low heat, till the potatoes are soft and the mince is cooked. Cool and keep aside.

Mix the flour, 3 eggs, milk, butter and salt with a little water to make a thin batter. Make thin pancakes / crepes on a flat pan cooking them on one side only.

Place each pan cake / crepe on a plate, add a tablespoon of the cooked mince on one end and roll up tucking in the sides as you would a spring roll. Follow the same procedure till all the mince and pancakes are exhausted. Heat the oil in a pan. Dip each Panthras / Pan Roll in the beaten egg then roll in bread crumbs. Shallow fry a few Pathras at a time, until golden. Serve with tomato or chillie sauce

52. SWEET PANTHRAS / FRIED COCONUT PAN ROLLS

Serves 6   Time required: 1 hour

Ingredients for the Pan Rolls
2 cups flour
3 eggs beaten
1 cup milk
2 tablespoons melted butter
A pinch salt
2 cups grated coconut sweetened with 2 tablespoons sugar
1 egg lightly beaten
Oil for deep frying
1 cup dry bread crumbs

Mix the flour, 3 eggs, milk, butter and salt with a little water to make a thin batter. Make thin pancakes / crepes on a flat pan cooking them on one side only.

Place each pan cake / crepe on a plate, add a tablespoon of the sweetened grated coconut on one end and roll up tucking in the sides as you would a spring roll. Follow the same procedure till all the grated coconut and pancakes are exhausted.

Heat the oil in a pan. Dip each Panthras / Pan Roll in the beaten egg then roll in bread crumbs. Shallow fry each until golden and Serve hot at Tea time or as a dessert.
Note: For a slight variation in taste, you could use jaggery or brown sugar instead of castor sugar.

X

THE ANGLO-INDIAN FESTIVE HAMPER

The Christmas season officially begins with the Baking of the Christmas Cakes a few weeks ahead of Christmas. Over the weeks leading up to Christmas, the cakes are regularly drenched with brandy or rum. Most Anglo-Indian families have their own recipe for the traditional Christmas cake, which is usually handed down through generations. Candied fruit, plums, currants, raisins, orange peel, nuts, etc are dexterously cut and chopped and soaked in Rum or Brandy a few weeks in advance. The whole family comes together to make the Christmas Cakes. Jobs are allotted to everyone - one to whip up the eggs, while another creams the butter and sugar, the flour is sieved, cake tins are lined, and a strong pair of arms are requisitioned to do the final mixing and stirring. After the cake batter is poured into the tins, the real fun starts with everyone fighting to lick the leftover batter in the mixing bowl and from the spoons and spatulas!!

Besides the Christmas Cakes, simple and easy recipes for lots of other old popular Anglo-Indian Christmas Sweets and Goodies such as Kalkals, Rose Cookies, Guava Cheese, Coconut Sweets etc are featured in this section.

A. CAKES & BAKES

1. CHRISTMAS FRUIT CAKE

Serves 6   Time required: 1 hour

Ingredients
300 grams plain flour or maida
¼ teaspoon salt
250 grams butter
250 grams sugar (powdered)
300 grams mixed dried fruit (chopped into small pieces and soaked in rum for 2 months)
1 teaspoon finely grated orange rind
3 eggs beaten well
½ cup cold milk
1 teaspoon vanilla essence
1 teaspoon baking powder

Preheat the oven to 200 Degrees C

Remove the soaked dry fruits and nuts from the rum and mix with 3 tablespoons of flour

Sift the flour, baking powder and salt together in a big bowl.
Cream the butter and sugar together till creamy. Add the eggs, chopped dry fruits and nuts that are mixed with flour, grated orange rind and Vanilla essence. Mix well. Slowly fold in the flour and mix gently. If the Batter is too thick add the milk. When evenly mixed, pour the mixture into a greased and papered cake tin and bake in a moderate oven (200 Degrees C) for 45 minutes to one hour or till the cake is cooked inside and brown on the top.

2. SIMPLE PLUM CAKE

Serves 6   Time required: 1 hour

Ingredients
300 grams flour or Maida
250 grams butter
250 grams powdered sugar
3 eggs (whites beaten well separately)
1 teaspoon baking powder
2 teaspoons chopped orange or lemon peel
100 grams black currants chopped
2 tablespoons date syrup (for colour)
2 cloves and 2 small pieces of cinnamon powdered
1teaspoon vanilla essence
¼ teaspoon salt

Preheat the oven to 200 Degrees C

Sift the flour, baking powder and salt together. Dust the orange / lemon peel and chopped black currants with a little flour. Cream the butter and sugar well. Add the egg yolks, date syrup, cinnamon and clove powder and vanilla essence and mix well. Add the orange / lemon peel and black currants. Slowly add the egg whites and flour and fold in well. If the mixture is too thick add a little milk. Pour into a greased and papered baking tin or dish and bake in a moderate oven (180 Degrees C) for about 40 to 45 minutes. (Or until a wooden toothpick comes out clean). Remove from the oven when done and set aside to cool.

3. RICH PLUM CAKE

Serves 6   Time required: 1 hour

Ingredients for the Cake
300 grams Plain Flour / Maida
300 grams brown Sugar
100 grams powdered white sugar
3 Eggs beaten

2 teaspoons vanilla essence
300 grams butter
1 teaspoon nutmeg powder
1 teaspoon cinnamon powder
3 tablespoons date syrup
300 grams dried fruit
50 grams orange /lemon peel
250 ml Rum or Brandy

Soak the dried fruit and orange / lemon peel in Rum or Brandy for about 1month. Just before using, strain and mix in 3 tablespoons of flour to it. Keep aside.

Preheat the oven to 200 Degrees C

Cream the butter, sugar and brown sugar well. Add the beaten eggs, date syrup and vanilla essence and mix well. Add the orange or lemon peel and dried fruits, nutmeg powder and cinnamon powder and mix well Slowly add the flour and fold in well. If the mixture is too thick add a little milk. Pour into a greased and papered baking tin or dish and bake in a moderate oven (180 Degrees C) for about 40 to 45 minutes (or until a wooden toothpick comes out clean).. Remove from the oven when done and set aside to cool.

Feed this cake with 2 or 3 tablespoons of rum or brandy every alternate day till just before Christmas. Then leave aside to let the cake absorb the liquor.

4. TRADITIONAL CHRISTMAS CAKE
WITH ALMOND AND ROYAL ICING

Serves 6   Time required: 1 hour

Ingredients
500 grams mixed dried fruits (equal quantities of currants, raisins and sultanas) chopped well and soaked in rum before hand
500 grams plain flour or maida
300 grams soft brown sugar

200 grams soft white sugar (powdered)
¼ teaspoon salt
2 teaspoons cinnamon powder
100 grams chopped orange or lemon peel
3 tablespoons date syrup or caramel syrup
500 grams butter
3 eggs beaten well
4 tablespoons milk
½ teaspoon baking powder

Preheat the oven to 200 Degrees C

Sift the flour, salt, baking powder and cinnamon powder in a bowl.

Cream the butter, white sugar and brown sugar well. Add the beaten eggs, date syrup / caramel syrup and vanilla essence and mix well. Add the orange or lemon peel and dried fruits, nutmeg powder and cinnamon powder and mix well. Slowly add the flour and fold in well. If the mixture is too thick add a little milk. Pour into a greased and papered baking tin or dish and bake in a moderate oven (180 Degrees C) for about 40 to 45 minutes. more (or until a wooden toothpick comes out clean). Remove from the oven when done and set aside to cool.

Feed this cake with 2 or 3 tablespoons of rum or brandy every alternate day till just before Christmas. Then leave aside to let the cake absorb the liquor.

Frost this cake just before Christmas as under:

Prepare Almond icing as follows:

Soak the 300 grams almonds in water overnight then grind to a thick paste. Add 500 grams Icing sugar, 1 egg yolk, 1 teaspoon almond essence and 2 tablespoons lime juice and cook with a little water in a heavy bottom pan till it solidifies. Remove from heat and cool. Knead it into a stiff ball. Roll out to fit the cake. (Brush some egg white all over the icing if desired). Spread a thin layer of jam on the cake to keep the icing in place. Place the layer of Almond Icing over the cake and press gently so that the entire cake is covered with the icing. Let it set for 2 days in the fridge.

If desired cover this layer with Royal Icing for a hard surface.

To prepare the Royal Icing sift 200 grams icing sugar into a bowl. Beat two egg whites then fold them into the sugar. Add 3 tablespoons of lemon juice and ½ teaspoon vanilla essence. Mix to a stiff consistency. Keep aside

Brush the cake with a layer of Jam or Egg white to help the icing stick to the cake. Add a thin layer of the Almond icing over the cake, pressing it gently to cover the whole cake. Using a flat spatula dipped in water spread the Royal icing over the layer of Almond icing. Decorate the cake as desired.

5. CHRISTMAS RUM AND RAISIN CAKE

Serves 6   Time required: 1 hour

Ingredients
500 grams refined flour or Maida
300 grams soft brown sugar
100 grams powdered white sugar
¼ teaspoon salt
2 teaspoons cinnamon powder
1teaspoon nutmeg powder
200 grams chopped black currants
200 grams chopped raisins
100 grams chopped sultanas
100 grams chopped orange / lemon peel
500 ml Rum or Brandy
250 ml Wine
500 grams butter
4 eggs beaten well
4 tablespoons milk
1 teaspoon baking powder
1 teaspoon vanilla essence
1 teaspoon almond essence

Cut and mix all the dried fruit together and soak in rum / brandy and wine for at least a month. When required drain and keep aside. Reserve the leftover liquor

Preheat the oven to 200 Degrees C
Sift the flour, baking powder and salt together. Dust the soaked dry fruit / peel with a little flour.

Cream the butter, sugar and brown sugar well. Add the beaten eggs, almond essence and vanilla essence and mix well. Add the orange / lemon peel and dried fruits, nutmeg powder and cinnamon powder and mix thoroughly. Slowly add the flour and fold in well. If the mixture is too thick add a little milk.

Pour into a greased and papered baking tins or dishes and bake in a moderate oven (180 Degrees C) for about one hour or more (or until a wooden toothpick comes out clean). Remove from the oven when done. Prick the cake with a toothpick and pour the remaining rum over it. Remove from the tin when cold and wrap tightly in foil or waxed paper and keep in an airtight container for the cake to absorb the rum. Just before serving, heat for a minute in a microwave oven and pour some more rum on the cake while hot. Tastes delicious!!!!!

6. CHOCOLATE YULE LOG CAKE

Serves 6   Time required: 1 hour

Ingredients
200 grams flour / maida
4 eggs beaten
250 grams sugar powdered
3 tablespoons Icing sugar
200 grams sugar
3 tablespoons cocoa powder
2 teaspoon Nescafe or any other Instant Coffee
125 grams fresh cream
50 grams chopped walnuts
1 teaspoon baking powder
½ teaspoon salt

Preheat the oven to 200 Degrees C

Sift the cocoa powder, Nescafe / Instant Coffee, flour and baking powder together. Cream the butter and sugar together well. Add the eggs one by one and mix well. Add the vanilla essence. Now add the sifted flour with the other ingredients and fold in the mixture to form a smooth slightly thick consistency without lumps. Pour into a greased and papered long cake tin and bake in a moderate oven (180 Degrees C) for 30 to 35 minutes (Or until a wooden toothpick comes out clean). Remove from the cake tin and turn it out on a sheet of paper, which has been liberally sprinkled with icing sugar. Roll the cake tightly with this paper so as to form a log and keep aside to cool.

Beat the fresh cream with 3 tablespoons of icing sugar and 2 tablespoons of cocoa powder till peaks form. Unroll the log cake from the paper and place on a suitable plate. Using a spatula, cover the cake with the icing. Then with a wet fork make long lines across the surface of the icing to create a bark effect on the log. Leave in the refrigerator until required for serving. Before serving, dust with icing sugar and decorate with some small leaves etc.

7. WALNUT CAKE

Serves 6   Time required: 1 hour

Ingredients
200 grams plain flour / maida
200 grams sugar
150 grams walnuts chopped
4 eggs beaten
1 tablespoon baking powder
100 grams honey
250 grams butter

Preheat the oven to 200 Degrees C
Sieve flour / maida with the baking powder Cream the butter and sugar together till creamy. Add the beaten eggs, walnuts and honey and mix well. Fold in the flour slowly. If the mixture is too thick add a little milk.

Pour into a greased and papered baking tin or dish and bake in a moderate oven (180 Degrees C) for about 40 to 45 minutes. (Or until a wooden toothpick comes out clean). Remove from the oven when done and set aside to cool.

8. ALMOND BRANDY CAKE

Serves 6   Time required: 1 hour

Ingredients
200 grams flour / maida
200 grams sugar
200 grams butter
¼ teaspoon salt
1 teaspoon baking powder
3 eggs beaten
2 teaspoons almond essence
2 teaspoons grated orange zest or orange peel
150 grams thinly sliced almonds
6 tablespoons brandy

Preheat the oven to 200 Degrees C
Cream the butter and sugar well. Add the beaten eggs, orange zest or orange peel, sliced almonds, brandy and almond essence and mix well. Slowly add the flour and fold in well. If the mixture is too thick add a little milk. Pour into a greased and papered baking tin or dish and bake in a moderate oven (180 Degrees C) for about 40 to 45 minutes. (Or until a wooden toothpick comes out clean). Remove from the oven when done and set aside to cool.

9. OLD FASHIONED POUND CAKE

Serves 6   Time required: 1 hour

Ingredients
250 grams refined flour / maida
250 grams butter

250 grams sugar
4 eggs beaten
1 teaspoon baking powder
2 teaspoons vanilla essence
¼ teaspoon salt

Preheat the oven to 200 Degrees C
Mix butter, sugar and eggs and beat well together. Sieve the flour with the salt and baking powder and fold into the butter mixture. Mix well. Then pour into a buttered and floured cake tin. Bake in a pre-heated oven for 35 to 40 minutes. (Or until a wooden toothpick comes out clean).

10. BUTTER SPONGE CAKE

Serves 6   Time required: 1 hour

Ingredients
300 grams refined flour or Maida
200 grams powdered sugar
250 grams butter
4 eggs beaten well
½ cup milk
1teaspoon baking powder
1teaspoon vanilla essence

Preheat the oven to 200 Degrees C
Sift the flour and baking powder together. Cream the butter and sugar together. Add the beaten eggs and vanilla essence and mix well. Fold in the flour a little at a time. Add milk if the mixture is too thick. Pour into a greased and floured cake tin and bake moderate oven (180 Degrees C) for 40 to 45 minutes (Or until a wooden toothpick comes out clean). Cool and then remove from the tin.

11. OLDEN DAYS SEED CAKE

Serves 6   Time required: 1 hour

Ingredients
250 grams butter
250 grams refined flour or Maida
250 grams sugar (powdered)
5 eggs beaten well
1 teaspoon baking powder
1 teaspoon cake seeds

Preheat the oven to 200 Degrees C
Sift the flour and baking powder together. Cream the butter and sugar well. Add the beaten eggs and mix well. Slowly add the flour and fold in the mixture Add the cake seeds and mix well. Pour into a buttered and floured cake tin and bake moderate oven (180 Degrees C) for 40 to 45 minutes. (Or until a wooden toothpick comes out clean).

12. SPONGE CAKE WITH BUTTER ICING

Serves 6   Time required: 1 hour

Ingredients
250 grams refined flour or Maida
200 grams powdered sugar
250 grams butter
4 eggs beaten well
½ cup milk (optional)
1 teaspoon baking powder
1 teaspoon vanilla essence

Preheat the oven to 200 Degrees C
Sift the flour and baking powder together. Cream the butter and sugar together. Add the beaten eggs and vanilla essence and mix well. Fold in the flour a little at a time. Add milk if the mixture is too thick. Pour into a greased and floured cake tin and bake in a moderate oven (180 Degrees C) for 40 to 45 minutes. (Or until a wooden toothpick comes

out clean). Set aside to cool. Frost the cake with Butter Icing only when completely cold.

TO MAKE THE BUTTER ICING

Beat 200 grams butter and 500 grams icing sugar together until creamy. Add 2 teaspoons vanilla essence and 2 drops pink or green food colour. Using a spatula, cover the cake with the butter icing, then with a wet fork make soft peaks across the surface of the icing. Decorate as desired

13. MARBLE CAKE

Serves 6   Time required: 1 hour

Ingredients
250 grams refined flour or Maida
1 teaspoon baking powder
250 grams butter
200 grams sugar powdered
4 tablespoons milk
A pinch of salt
1 teaspoon vanilla essence
4 eggs beaten well
2 tablespoons cocoa powder

Preheat the oven to 200 Degrees C
Sift the flour, salt and baking powder together. Cream the butter and sugar well. Gradually add the eggs and mix well. Add the vanilla essence. Fold in the flour slowly. Add milk if the mixture is too thick. Divide the mixture into 2 portions. Mix the cocoa powder with a teaspoon of milk and add to one portion of the mixture. Mix well. In a greased and papered cake tin, pour alternate tablespoonfuls of the plain and chocolate mixture till both mixtures are used up. Bake the marble cake in a moderate oven (180 Degrees C) for about 1 hour. (Or until a wooden toothpick comes out clean).

14. DARK CHOCOLATE CAKE

Serves 6   Time required: 1 hour

Ingredients
250 grams flour / maida
250 grams sugar
3 eggs beaten
4 tablespoons cocoa powder
1 cup plain curds / yogurt
½ cup sunflower oil
1 teaspoon soda bicarbonate (baking soda)
1 teaspoon vanilla essence
½ cup milk

Preheat the oven to 200 Degrees C
Break the eggs in a bowl and whisk well. Add the curds / yogurt, oil, sugar, vanilla essence and soda bicarbonate and beat well. Add the cocoa powder and mix well. Fold in the flour. Add a little milk if batter is too thick. Pour into a greased baking dish or tin and bake in a moderate oven (180 Degrees C) for 40 to 45 minutes. (Or until a wooden toothpick comes out clean)

15. RICH CHOCOLATE CAKE WITH CHOCOLATE ICING

Serves 6   Time required: 1 hour

Ingredients
250 grams plain flour or Maida
50 grams cocoa powder
200 grams sugar powdered
250 grams butter
5 eggs
2 teaspoons Instant Coffee
1 teaspoon vanilla essence
2 level teaspoons baking powder

Preheat the oven to 200 Degrees C
Sift the cocoa powder, Instant coffee, flour and baking powder together. Cream the butter and sugar together well. Add the eggs one by one and mix well. Add the vanilla essence. Now add the sifted flour with the other ingredients and fold in the mixture to form a smooth slightly thick consistency without lumps. Add a little milk if the batter is too thick. Pour into a greased and papered baking dish or cake tin and bake in a moderate oven (180 Degrees C) for 40 to 45 minutes. (Or until a wooden toothpick comes out clean). Set aside to cool. Frost the cake with Chocolate Icing only when completely cold

TO MAKE THE CHOCOLATE ICING
Beat 6 tablespoons butter and 500 grams sifted icing sugar together until creamy. Add, 1 teaspoon vanilla essence, ¼ teaspoon salt and 2 tablespoons cocoa powder and stir until smooth. Using a spatula, cover the cake with Chocolate Icing. Decorate as desired.

16. CHOCOLATE RUM CAKE WITH FRESH CREAM

Serves 6   Time required: 1 hour

Ingredients
250 Grams Plain Flour / Maida
250 grams soft brown sugar
3 Eggs Beaten
3 tablespoons cocoa
1 teaspoon baking powder
1 cup sunflower oil or any other cooking oil
½ cup milk
1 teaspoon vanilla essence
6 tablespoons Rum
200 grams fresh cream
3 tablespoons icing sugar
10 walnut halves

Preheat the oven to 200 Degrees C
Sift flour, cocoa and baking powder into bowl. Mix in the brown sugar. Add the beaten eggs, rum, oil, a little milk, and vanilla essence and mix

well to a smooth batter. Pour into a greased and papered cake tin and bake for 1 hour in a moderate oven (180 Degrees C) or until the case has risen well and brown on top. Set aside to cool then remove from the tin.

Beat the Cream, Icing sugar and the remaining milk until thick and creamy. Pile on top of the cake and smoothen with a spatula. Decorate with the walnut halves.

17. HOME MADE CHOCOLATE BROWNIES

Serves 6   Time required: 1 hour

Ingredients
200 grams plain flour / maida
2 eggs
200 grams powdered sugar
200 grams butter
A pinch of salt
2 tablespoons cocoa powder
1 teaspoon vanilla essence
2 tablespoons broken cashew nuts of walnuts

Preheat the Oven to 200 Degrees C
Beat the butter, sugar, eggs, salt, cocoa powder and vanilla essence together till creamy. Add the flour and mix well. If mixture is too thick add a little milk. Pour the mixture into a buttered and floured cake tin and sprinkle the broken cashew nuts or walnuts on the top. Bake in a moderate oven (180 Degrees C) for 30 to 40 minutes in a moderate oven. The top should be brown and crisp.

18. LEMON CAKE

Serves 6   Time required: 1 hour

Ingredients
300 grams plain flour or maida
4 eggs
200 grams sugar powdered

200 grams butter
1 teaspoon baking powder
¼ teaspoon salt
2 tablespoons fresh lime juice or cream of tartar
1 teaspoon vanilla essence
1 tablespoon grated lemon rind

Preheat the oven to 200 Degrees C
Sift the flour, salt and baking powder together. Cream the butter and sugar together in a suitable bowl. Add the beaten eggs, lime juice or cream of tartar, lemon rind and vanilla essence and mix well. Fold in the flour a little at a time. Add a little milk if the mixture is too thick. Pour into a greased and floured cake tin and bake in a moderate oven (180 Degrees C) for 40 to 45 minutes. (Or until a wooden toothpick comes out clean).

For the Lemon Topping: Whip together 100 grams fresh cream, 100 grams icing sugar, ½ teaspoon vanilla essence, ¼ teaspoon lemon food colour and 2 tablespoons lime juice till creamy. Pile on top of the cake and spread with a spatula. Decorate as desired. Refrigerate and serve when required.

19. SIMPLE COFFEE CAKE

Serves 6   Time required: 1 hour

Ingredients
250 grams plain flour or Maida
50 grams Instant Coffee
200 grams sugar powdered
250 grams butter
5 eggs
1 teaspoon vanilla essence
2 level teaspoons baking powder
3 tablespoons icing sugar

Preheat the oven to 200 Degrees C
Sift the Instant coffee, flour and baking powder together. Cream the butter and sugar together well. Add the eggs one by one and mix well. Add the

vanilla essence. Slowly add the sifted flour with all the other ingredients and fold in the mixture to form a smooth slightly thick consistency without lumps. Add a little milk if necessary. Pour into a greased and papered baking dish or cake tin and bake in a moderate oven (180 Degrees C) for 40 to 45 minutes. (Or until a wooden toothpick comes out clean). When still hot, sprinkle the icing sugar on top.

20. COCONUT CAKE

Serves 6   Time required: 1 hour

Ingredients
250 grams plain flour or Maida
50 grams desiccated coconut
200 grams powdered sugar
250 grams butter
4 eggs beaten
½ teaspoon salt
1teaspoon vanilla essence
2 level teaspoons baking powder

Preheat the oven to 200 Degrees C

Sift salt, flour and baking powder together. Cream the butter and sugar together well. Add the eggs, desiccated coconut and vanilla essence and mix well. Slowly add the sifted flour and fold in the mixture to form a smooth slightly thick consistency without lumps. Add a little milk if the mixture is too thick. Pour into a greased and papered baking dish or cake tin and bake in a moderate oven (180 Degrees C) for about one hour. (Or until a wooden toothpick comes out clean). Cool and remove from the tin.

21. BOLE CAKE OR SEMOLINA CAKE

Bole Cake also known as Bolo de Baatica or Baarth Cake is another legacy of the Portuguese to Anglo-Indian Cuisine. Traditionally made at Christmas in the olden days, the earlier recipes called for '2 wineglasses of sherry'! This cake is mainly made of semolina instead of flour which gives an exotic flavor to this cake.

Serves 6   Time required: 1 hour

Ingredients
300 grams semolina or soogi
1 cup milk
200 grams butter
150 grams sugar powdered
5 eggs beaten well
100 grams blanched and chopped almonds
½ teaspoon baking powder
1teaspoon vanilla essence
2 tablespoons rosewater (optional)
4 tablespoons Brandy (optional)
Preheat the oven to 200 Degrees C

Roast the semolina with a little ghee or butter for about 8 to 10 minutes on low heat till it gives out a nice aroma. Mix it with all the other ingredients to form a smooth batter without lumps. Pour into a greased and floured flat tin and bake in a moderate oven (180 Degrees C) for 40 minutes. (Or until a wooden toothpick comes out clean). Cool and remove from the tin.

22. SEMOLINA, COCONUT AND RAISIN CAKE

Serves 6   Time required: 1 hour

Ingredients
200 grams semolina or soogi
1 cup milk
200 grams butter or Margarine
200 grams sugar powdered
4 eggs beaten well
½ teaspoon baking powder
200 grams desiccated coconut
1teaspoon vanilla essence
½ teaspoon salt
100 grams raisins

Preheat the oven to 200 Degrees C

Roast the semolina with a little ghee or butter for about 8 to 10 minutes on low heat till it gives out a nice aroma. Cream the butter / margarine and sugar well. Add the eggs, desiccated coconut, salt and vanilla essence and mix well. Slowly add the roasted semolina, and fold in the mixture to form a smooth slightly thick consistency without lumps. Mix in the raisins. Add a little milk if the mixture is too thick. Pour into a greased and papered baking dish or cake tin and bake in a moderate oven (180 Degrees C) for about one hour. (Or until a wooden toothpick comes out clean). Cool and remove from the tin.

23. BANANA AND WALNUT CAKE

Serves 6   Time required: 1 hour

Ingredients
200 grams flour
150 grams sugar powdered
50 grams chopped walnuts
3 eggs beaten
½ teaspoon salt
3 tablespoons milk
150 grams butter
3 large ripe bananas (Yellow skin variety) Mashed well
2 teaspoons baking powder

Preheat the oven to 200 Degrees C

Sift the flour, baking powder and salt together. Cream the butter and sugar well. Mix in the mashed banana, milk and walnuts. Fold in the flour. If the mixture is too thick add a little more milk. Pour the batter in a greased baking dish and bake in a moderate oven (180 Degrees C) for about 30 minutes. (Or until a wooden toothpick comes out clean). Remove from the oven and cool.

24. MATRIMONY CAKE OR LOVE CAKE

Serves 6   Time required: 1 hour

Ingredients
300 grams lightly roasted semolina / soogi
200 grams butter or margarine
6 eggs beaten well
200 grams sugar
200 grams cashew nuts broken into bits
100 grams honey
2 tablespoons rose water (optional)
¼ teaspoon nutmeg
½ teaspoon cinnamon powder
2 tablespoons zest of orange or lime
¼ teaspoon salt
1 teaspoon baking powder
1 teaspoon vanilla essence
3 tablespoons icing Sugar for garnish
3 tablespoons Rum or Brandy

Preheat oven to 200°C.

Cream the butter / margarine and sugar well. Add all the above ingredients (except the Icing sugar) and mix well to form a smooth slightly thick consistency without lumps. Add a little milk if the mixture is too thick. Pour into a greased and papered baking dish or cake tin and bake in a moderate oven (180 Degrees C) for about one hour. (Or until a wooden toothpick comes out clean).
Cool and remove from the tin. Dust with icing sugar and cut into slices to serve.

25. MARMALADE ROLL

Serves 6   Time required: 1 hour

Ingredients
250 grams flour / maida
250 grams butter 200 grams sugar

3 eggs beaten
½ teaspoon baking powder
1 teaspoon orange essence
2 tablespoons milk
3 tablespoons marmalade
¼ teaspoon salt

Preheat the oven to 200 Degrees C
Sift the flour, salt and baking powder together. Cream the butter and sugar together in a suitable bowl. Add the beaten eggs, orange essence and mix well. Fold in the flour a little at a time. Add a little milk if the mixture is too thick. Pour into a greased and floured cake tin and bake in a moderate oven (180 Degrees C) for 40 to 50 minutes. (Or until a wooden toothpick comes out clean).
Take a sheet of thick brown paper and sprinkle a little water on it. Sprinkle sugar liberally on it. While the cake is still hot, turn it out on to the dampened paper. Cut it horizontally in the center without going to the ends and open it out so that it becomes a square. Spread warm marmalade on it then roll it tightly with the paper to form a roll. Chill in the refrigerator for about 2 hours. When required cut into round slices and serve.

B. CHRISTMAS GOODIES & SWEETS

1. TRADITIONAL CHRISTMAS PLUM PUDDING

Serves 6   Time required: 1 hour

Ingredients
200 grams fresh bread crumbs
200 grams butter
2 teaspoons instant coffee (Nescafe or Bru)
2 teaspoons golden or date syrup
½ teaspoon baking powder
2 eggs beaten well

¼ cup rum
1 teaspoon ground cinnamon and cloves
¼ teaspoon ground nutmeg
100 grams raisins
100 grams chopped sultanas
100 grams mixed peel
½ teaspoon salt
100 grams sugar

Cream the butter and sugar together then add the eggs and mix well. Gradually add all the other ingredients and mix well. Grease a Pudding Mould or any suitable bowl with butter. Pour the pudding mixture into it then steam the pudding for about 1 hour on low heat till it is firm to touch *Note: This pudding can be made in advance and refrigerated till required. Steam for 10 minute or microwave for 3 minutes before serving. For a more exotic taste, when still warm make a few small holes all over the pudding and pour about 6 tablespoons of rum over it.*

2. TRADITIONAL CHRISTMAS FRUIT MINCE PIES

Serves 6   Time required: 1 hour

Ingredients
200 grams flour / maida
150 grams butter
A pinch of salt
2 eggs beaten
100 grams powdered sugar
½ teaspoon baking powder
1 teaspoon cinnamon powder
250 grams chopped dry fruits soaked in a little rum before hand

Preheat the oven to 200 Degrees C

Sift the flour with the baking powder, cinnamon powder and salt. Make a soft dough with the flour, butter, eggs and a little water. Cover and leave aside for one hour.

Roll out the dough and cut out circles with a small saucer. Line a few pie shells with this. Fill each lined pie shell with the marinated dry fruit. Now seal each pie with another circle of the dough. Press down firmly. Prick on top with a toothpick.

Beat 1 small egg and brush the tops of the pies. Bake for 20 minutes (200 Degrees C) until golden. Leave to cool, then remove to a wire rack.

To serve, lightly dust with icing sugar.

3. KALKALS / KULKULS (FRIED SWEETENED BALLS OF DOUGH)

Serves 6   Time required: 1 hour 30 minutes

Ingredients
I kg plain flour or maida
6 eggs beaten well
2 cups thick coconut milk
½ teaspoon salt
300 grams sugar
1 teaspoon baking powder
Oil for deep frying

Mix the flour, salt, sugar and baking powder together. Add the coconut milk and eggs and knead to a soft dough. Keep aside for an hour. Form kalkals by taking small lumps of the dough and roll on the back of a fork or a wooden kalkal mould, to form a scroll. Alternately, roll out the dough and cut into fancy shapes with kalkal or cookie cutters. Heat oil in a deep pan and fry as many kalkals as possible at a time. Keep aside.

To frost the kalkals, melt 1 cup of sugar with ½ cup of water and one teaspoon vanilla essence. When the sugar syrup crystallizes pour over the kalkals and mix well.
Store the Kalkals in airtight boxes when cold.

4. ROSE COOKIES / ROSA COOKIES

Serves 6   Time required: 1 hour

Ingredients
½ kg plain flour or maida
100 grams rice flour or very fine soogi (optional)
1 cup coconut milk
200 grams sugar
6 eggs beaten well
½ teaspoon salt
1 litre oil for frying
1 teaspoon vanilla essence
1 teaspoon baking powder

Mix all the ingredients together to form a smooth slightly thick batter. Heat oil in a deep pan till it reaches boiling point. Now place the rose cookie mould into the oil to get hot. When the mould is hot enough dip it half way only into the batter and put it back immediately into the boiling oil. Shake the mould to separate the cookie from it. Heat the mould again and repeat the process. Fry rose cookies till brown. Continue in this way till the batter is finished.

Note: The batter will stick to the rose cookie mould with a hissing sound only if it is sufficiently hot otherwise it will just slide off the mould

5. MARSHMALLOWS

Makes 30 pieces   Time required: 1 hour

Ingredients
2 tablespoons gelatin
1 teaspoon vanilla essence
200 grams sugar
2 tablespoons Icing sugar
¼ teaspoon pink food colour

Soak the gelatin in ½ cup cold water and keep aside for some time till it dissolves completely. Meanwhile on low heat, melt the sugar with ½ cup of water in a pan. Add the dissolved gelatin mixture, mix well and bring to boil. Keep cooking on high heat for about 6 to 8 minutes without stirring. Remove from heat and allow to cool. When it is still lukewarm, add the vanilla essence and the food colour and beat well with a fork or egg-beater until thick. Pour this mixture into a dish or plate that has been rinsed with cold water. Refrigerate till set. Cut into squares then roll in Icing Sugar.

6. MARZIPAN SWEETS

Makes 30 pieces   Time required: 1 hour

Ingredients
250 grams almonds
250 grams sugar
300 grams icing sugar
2 egg whites
A little rose water for grinding
¼ teaspoon almond essence
250 grams cashew nuts

Grind the almonds and cashew nuts with the egg whites and rose water to a smooth paste. Transfer the paste into a heavy bottomed pan and add the sugar. Cook on low heat stirring all the time till the mixture forms a soft ball. Remove from heat and add the icing sugar. Divide the mixture into 3 parts and add a few drops of different food colour of your choice. Knead well. Divide each portion into even sized balls and mould into different shapes.

7. DOLDOL / DODOL (BLACK RICE HALWA)
This is the old fashioned way of making Doldol.

Makes 30 pieces   Time required: 2 hours to 3 hours

Ingredients
2 cups Black Puttu Rice flour / Black Rice flour

(if you can't get the Rice flour buy the black or purple rice and grind in a grinder /blender at home)
4 cups Coconut milk
½ teaspoon salt
2 teaspoons almond essence
6 dessertspoons ghee or butter
2 cups soft white sugar
100 grams sliced almonds

In a fairly big vessel, boil the sugar and coconut milk together till it forms a thick syrup. Add the Rice flour to the syrup a little at a time and mix well. Add the ghee, salt, almonds and almond essence. Stirring continuously, cook till the mixture is thick and leaves the sides of the pan. Stir in the sliced almonds. Remove from the heat and pour onto a greased plate. Cut into squares when cold. (The Dodol will be black)

The same recipe could be used to prepare Dodol / Doldol in the Microwave. Mix all the above ingredients together in a microwave safe bowl. Microwave the mixture on medium heat for 8 minutes. Remove from microwave and stir well. Repeat. The procedure 3 more times (totally 28 minutes) till it forms a jelly like mass. Mix till smooth, then pour onto a greased plate and allow it to cool then cut into squares.

8. CINNAMON DOUGH NUTS

Serves 6   Time required: 45 minutes
2 cups refined flour or maida
1 cup milk
2 tablespoons sugar
2 eggs beaten
1 teaspoon baking powder
2 teaspoons cinnamon powder
50 grams butter
Oil for frying
2 tablespoons Icing sugar for dusting

Make a soft dough with the flour, sugar, cinnamon powder, baking powder, milk, eggs and butter. Cover with a damp cloth and let it stand for 1 to 2 hours. Make small balls of the dough, flatten them and make a hole in the middle of each one. Heat oil in a pan till smoky. Fry the doughnuts/ fritters till golden brown. Remove from the oil and sprinkle Icing Sugar on the top.

9. BEBICA / BEVICA

Serves 6   Time required: 1 hour

Ingredients
1 cup rice flour
1 cup wheat flour
4 eggs
2 cups coconut milk
2 tablespoons butter
3 tablespoons sugar
1 teaspoon vanilla essence
3 tablespoons sliced almonds

Mix the rice flour and the wheat flour together.
Cream the butter and sugar together. Add the eggs and coconut milk and mix well. Slowly add the rice and wheat flour and vanilla essence and mix well to a smooth thick batter. Pour into a greased baking dish or tin and sprinkle the sliced almonds on the top. Bake at 200 Degrees C for about 40 minutes till the top gets brown. Remove and let it cool. When cold remove from the tin and cut into slices.

10. GUAVA CHEESE

Serves 6   Time required: 1 hour
6 ripe guavas preferably the pink variety
¾ cup sugar
50 grams unsalted butter
½ teaspoon vanilla essence
¼ cochineal food colouring

Wash and cut the guavas into quarters and boil them well in a little water till nice and soft. Mash well. Strain through a thin cloth and throw away the skin and seeds. Boil the strained thick juice with the sugar and keep on stirring till the mixture turns slightly thick. Add the butter, vanilla essence and cochineal. Simmer till nice and thick and the mixture starts leaving the sides of the pan. Pour onto a buttered plate. Cut into squares when cold.

11. COCONUT SWEET / COCONUT CANDY

Makes 30 pieces   Time required: 1 hour

Ingredients
2 cups grated coconut
3 cups sugar
1 cup milk
1 teaspoon ghee
½ teaspoon vanilla essence
½ teaspoon food colour either pink or green

Melt the sugar with the milk in a thick bottomed vessel. Add the grated coconut and mix well. Cook till the coconut is soft. Add the vanilla essence, pink or green food colour and ghee and mix well. Simmer on low heat till the mixture becomes thick and leaves the sides of the vessel. Pour on to a greased plate and cut into squares when slightly cold

12. MATRIMONY SWEET (SEMOLINA COCONUT SWEET)

Makes 30 pieces   Time required: 1 hour

Ingredients
2 cups grated coconut
1 cup roasted fine soogi / semolina
3 cups sugar
1 cup milk
½ cup condensed milk

1 teaspoon ghee
½ teaspoon vanilla essence
½ teaspoon food colour either pink or green

Roast the semolina with one teaspoon ghee till it gives out a nice aroma. Melt the sugar with the milk and condensed milk in a thick bottomed vessel. Add the grated coconut and mix well. Cook till the coconut is soft. Add the semolina, essence, food colour and ghee and mix well. Simmer on low heat till the mixture becomes thick and leaves the sides of the vessel. Pour on to a greased plate and cut into squares.

13. GROUNDNUT TOFFEE (PEANUT BRITTLE)

Makes 30 pieces   Time required: 1 hour

Ingredients
½ kg good white jaggery
300 grams crushed groundnuts or peanuts
1 teaspoon ghee

Melt the jaggery in a thick-bottomed vessel with about 1 cup of water till thick syrup is obtained. Add the crushed groundnuts and the ghee and cook on low heat stirring all the time, till the mixture forms a ball and leaves the sides of the vessel. Pour on to a greased plate and spread well with a wooden spoon or spatula. When slightly cool cut into squares.

14. CASHEW NUT TOFFEE

Makes 24 pieces   Time required: 45 minutes

Ingredients
½ kg good cashew nuts, broken into bits
250 grams sugar
2 teaspoons ghee

Powder the sugar and keep aside. Roast the cashew nuts lightly till just warm. Cool then dry grind in a blender till smooth.

In a thick-bottomed pan, melt the powdered sugar with ¼ cup water, boiling only once. Reduce heat and mix in the ground cashew nuts and ghee. Cook on low heat for 2 or 3 minutes till the mixture leaves the sides of the pan. Remove from heat and pour on to a greased plate. Flatten with a wooden spoon or rolling pin. Cut into squares or diamond shapes.

15. MILK TOFFEE

Makes 24 pieces   Time required: 1 hour

Ingredients
1 litre milk
500 grams sugar
½ teaspoon vanilla essence
1 teaspoon butter

Mix the milk and sugar together in a pan and cook on low heat till the sugar dissolves and the mixture turns thick. Keep stirring all the time till the mixture leaves the sides of the pan. Add the essence and butter and mix well. Pour onto a greased plate and cut into squares when still warm.

16. CHOCOLATE FUDGE

Makes 24 pieces   Time required: 1 hour

Ingredients
300 grams sugar
100 grams cocoa powder or Drinking Chocolate
200 grams plain flour / maida
4 tablespoons ghee
1 teaspoon vanilla essence

Heat the ghee in a pan and roast the flour over a low flame for a few minutes till it gives out a nice aroma stirring all the time. (Care should be taken not to burn it) The ghee and flour should look like thick paste. Keep aside.

Heat 2 cups of water in a suitable pan. When warm mix in the sugar, vanilla essence and cocoa powder. Simmer on low heat stirring continuously till a one thread consistency is reached. Add the roasted flour slowly and mix well to blend well with the sugar syrup. Continue to cook on low heat, stirring continuously till the mass thickens and leaves the sides of the pan. Pour onto to greased plate and smoothen. Cut into squares or diamond shapes when firm to touch and still slightly warm.

17. CHOCOLATE NUTTY FUDGE

Makes 24 pieces Preparation time 1 hour

Ingredients
300 grams sugar
100 grams cocoa powder
1 cup milk
3 tablespoons butter
1 teaspoon vanilla essence
100 grams chopped walnuts and cashew nuts

Heat the milk in a suitable pan. When warm mix in the sugar, vanilla essence and cocoa powder. Simmer on low heat stirring continuously. When the mixture starts leaving the sides of the pan, add the butter and chopped nuts and mix well. Remove from heat and pour onto a greased plate. Cut into squares or diamond shapes when slightly cool.

18. CHOCOLATE WALNUT SQUARES

Serves 6 Preparation time 1 hour

Ingredients
1 tin condensed milk
4 tablespoons drinking chocolate or cocoa powder
200 grams sugar powdered
100 grams chopped walnuts
2 tablespoons butter

Heat the sugar and condensed milk together in a thick bottomed pan till the sugar melts completely. Add the drinking chocolate / cocoa powder, butter and the walnuts and mix well. Simmer on low heat till the mixture thickens and leaves the sides of the vessel.

Pour onto a greased plate to set. When slightly cold cut into squares.

19. SUGARY CASHEW NUT MACAROONS

Serves 6 Preparation and Cooking Time: 1 hour

Ingredients
1 cup powdered sugar
½ cup tiny bits of cashew nuts
8 cardamoms powdered
2 egg whites

Beat the egg whites till stiff. Add the powdered sugar, cardamom powder and cashew nuts and mix well. Using a teaspoon place blobs of the batter 2 inches apart on a greased tray and bake at 200 Degrees C, for 30 minutes.

20. MILK DUMPLINGS

Serves 6   Time required: 1 hour

Ingredients
1 cup flour (maida)
1 litre milk
3 tablespoons sugar
½ teaspoon vanilla essence
1 cup coconut milk

Make a soft dough with the flour, 1 teaspoon sugar, a pinch of salt and a little water. Roll out the dough and cut into small diamond shapes or dumplings.

Boil the milk with the sugar in a sufficiently large vessel. Drop in the dumplings and add the vanilla essence. Simmer on low heat till the dumplings are cooked. Add coconut milk. Serve when cold.

C. HOME MADE WINES

The miracle of wine has always been associated with Divine Alchemy. Grape Wine is a sweet, turbid, sticky juice of fresh grapes rolled into an angry frothing mass by a powerful invisible force, which later subsides to reveal limpid nectar, bearing the gift of euphoria. The making of wine depends on the quantity of fermenting agent used, which controls the transformation of grape juice into the finest wine.

While there are many ways of making grape wine commercially, the recipe of making homemade grape wine is a standard one used over many years. Most families have their own recipe for making grape wine for Christmas.

Grape wine and ginger wine are the two wines that are normally prepared for Christmas. However the other wines that are featured here are easy to prepare and taste delicious as well.

1 GRAPE WINE

2 kg sweet black grapes
2 kg sugar
4 litres water
½ teaspoon active dry yeast

Wash the grapes and crush them well with the sugar. Add the water and the yeast and store in a stone jar or any other container. Leave for 21 days stirring the wine every alternate day.
Strain the wine into another jar after 21 days.

To add more colour to the wine, burn or caramelize some sugar with a little of the wine in a saucepan. When the sugar is caramelized to a nice brown, add to the wine and mix well. It will give it a lovely rich colour. Bottle and keep for future use.

For making larger quantities of wine increase the ingredients accordingly.

2. GINGER WINE

Ginger Wine is also known as O T or 'THE OTHER THING' - the Temperance Drink for Teetotalers. In the days of prohibition during the war, people were advised to drink non-temperance wines.

100 grams fresh ginger
1 kg sugar
6 limes (extract the juice)
3 pieces cinnamon
1 red chillie (remove the seeds)
4 litres water

Peel and wash the ginger and cut into thin slices. Make lime juice and keep aside.

In a large clean vessel, boil the fresh ginger, sugar, cinnamon and red chillies with 4 litres of water on low heat till the decoction is slightly thick. Remove from heat and add the lime juice. When cold, strain through a thin cloth, then bottle, and use whenever required. This wine will last for almost 3 months if kept in the fridge and is a good digestive.

3. TRADITIONAL MULLED WINE OR HOT TODDY

Mulled wine is a traditional drink during winter, especially around Christmas time and is usually made with red wine and Brandy together with various mulling spices and raisins. It is served hot or warm and may be alcoholic or non-alcoholic.

1 bottle Red Wine
1 cup Brandy
½ cup fresh orange juice
¼ cup sugar
8 whole cloves

3 pieces of cinnamon each about 1 inch long
2 star anise (optional)

Combine all the above ingredients together in a suitable saucepan and simmer on low heat for about 15 minutes. **(Do not boil)**
Serve warm in medium size Wine glasses

4. BEETROOT WINE

2 kg beetroot
1 kg sugar
1 cup fresh orange juice
½ cup lemon or lime juice
4 litres water
A small piece of ginger
½ teaspoon yeast
6 cloves

Peel and wash the beetroot and cut into pieces. Boil the beetroot in 4 litres water together with the ginger and cloves till the beetroot is soft. Mash well and allow to cool. Strain it and add the sugar, orange juice and limejuice. When cold pour into a stone jar. Spread the yeast on a slice of toasted bread and allow it to float in the liquid. Keep the jar closed for 14 days. Strain the wine into another vessel. Let it stand for a week then strain way the sediments and bottle.

5 GOOSEBERRY WINE

2 kg gooseberries (the star variety)
3 kg sugar
½ kg raisins minced finely
½ teaspoon cinnamon powder
1 teaspoon nutmeg powder
3 litres boiled and cooled water

Lightly crush the gooseberries. Mix all the ingredients together and store in a porcelain jar for 21 days stirring it every day. Strain the wine on the 22nd day. Add caramelized sugar to get the desired colour and bottle it. This wine should be used within a month.

6. RICE WINE

1 kg raw rice
1 kg sugar
500 grams raisins minced finely
5 litres boiling water
½ teaspoon yeast granules

Place the rice, sugar and raisins in a large vessel. Pour 5 litres of boiling water over them. Cover and let it remain lukewarm. Stir in the yeast. Leave for 3 weeks stirring every day. When the bubbles of fermentation stop, strain the wine and leave for a month before using

----

XI

HOME MADE CURRY POWDERS USED IN ANGLO-INDIAN COOKING

Here are a few recipes to make your own Homemade Curry Powders at home. Homemade powders always give a better taste to curries than store bought curry powders. Make small quantities and store in air tight bottles or jars for future use.

1. BASIC CHILLIE POWDER

½ kg Red Chilies (long or round variety for pungency)
½ kg Kashmiri Chilies or any other non spicy chillies (for adding colour)

Roast the two types of chilies in a pan or in a microwave oven for a few minutes. Powder them at home in the dry blender or get it done at the mill. *A teaspoon or two of this chillie powder could be used for any type of dish that calls for chillie powder. It can be stored for more than a year.*

2. ANGLO-INDIAN CURRY POWDER

250 grams Red Chillies for pungency
200 grams Kashmiri Chillies or any other chillies for colour
100 coriander seeds
100 grams cumin seeds

Roast all the above ingredients separately then mix altogether and grind to a fine powder either in a blender or mixer at home or get it ground in a mill.

A teaspoon or two of this powder can be used for almost all curries both vegetarian and non- vegetarian. It can be stored and used for more than a year.

3. PEPPER WATER POWDER

250 grams Red Chilies
50 grams pepper corns
50 grams cumin seeds
50 grams coriander seeds
20 grams turmeric powder

Roast all the above ingredients and then grind together to a powder.
2 teaspoons of this powder should be added to 2 cups of water, juice of 2 tomatoes, a lump of tamarind and a little salt and cooked for 5 minutes to make instant pepper water. This pepper water should be seasoned with mustard, garlic and curry leaves.

4. ALL SPICE POWDER (GARAM MASALA POWDER)

1 teaspoon pepper corns
1 tablespoon cloves
1 tablespoon cardamoms
3 (one inch) pieces of cinnamon
1 tablespoon fennel seeds (saunf)

Roast all the above lightly for a few minutes then dry grind to a fine powder.
A teaspoon of this spice powder can be used for any recipe that calls for all spice powder or garam masala.

5. VINDALOO CURRY POWDER / PASTE

25 grams mustard seeds
250 grams red chilies for pungency
50 grams cumin seeds
10 grams pepper corns

Roast all the above ingredients together for a few minutes then powder in a mill or dry grind in a blender.

Use 2 teaspoons of this powder for every ½ kg of meat when cooking Vindaloo along with the other ingredients as per the recipe. If this powder is stored in an airtight bottle it will stay fresh for more than a year. The same mixture can also be made into a paste if ground in vinegar but it should be stored in the fridge.

A. WEIGHTS AND MEASURES

The old fashioned house hold way of measuring ingredients using cups and spoons are more convenient and helpful while cooking rather than weighing the ingredients on a weighing scale. However a few precautions have to be taken while measuring

1. While using a cup to measure dry ingredients, fill the cup a little more than full then pass the edge of a knife over the top to level it off.

2. While measuring flour, always measure the flour after sifting it and the flour should not be pressed down in the cup.

3. For measuring ghee, melt the ghee before measuring in the cup.

(1) APPROXIMATE EQUIVALENT MEASURES IN KILOS & GRAMS

A few grains	-	About ¼ teaspoon
A dash of liquid	-	A few drops
60 drops	-	1 teaspoon
2 teaspoons	-	1 dessertspoon
3 Teaspoons	-	1 Tablespoon
4 Tablespoons	-	¼ Tea Cup
16 Tablespoons	-	1 Tea Cup
3 Tea Cups	-	1 Litre
1 Litre	-	1 ¾ Pint
2 Measuring Cups	-	1 Pint
4 Tea Cups	-	1 Pint
1 Rounded Teaspoon	-	5 Grams
1 Rounded Tablespoon	-	14 Gram
250 Grams	-	¼ Kg
500 Grams	-	½ Kg
1000 Grams	-	1 Kg
4 Tea cups flour	-	600 grams
1 Tea cup sugar	-	200 grams
2 ¾ Tea cups rice	-	1 kilogram

2 Tea cups butter	-	900 grams
1 Tea cup chopped nuts	-	150 grams
2 ½ Tea Cups dried fruit	-	500 grams
1 tea cup bread crumbs	-	50 grams

(2) APPROXIMATE EQUIVALENT MEASURES IN POUNDS AND OUNCES

1 oz	-	2 tablespoons
2 ozs	-	30 grams
2.2 lbs	-	1 kg
20 ozs	-	1 pint
1 lb sugar	-	21/2 measuring cups
1 lb dry fruits chopped	-	3 measuring cups
40 ozs	-	1 quart or 2 pints
5 0zs milk or water	-	1 tea cupful
6 ozs milk or water	-	1 tumbler
6 ozs sugar	-	1 tea cup
4 ozs flour	-	1 teacup pressed well
1 oz ghee or butter	-	4 teaspoons
1 oz sugar	-	4 teaspoons
1 oz maida	-	6 teaspoons
8 ozs ghee	-	1 measuring cup

B. OVEN TEMPERATURES

TYPE	o F	o C	GAS MARK
COOL OVEN	225o	120o	½ TO 1
VERY SLOW OVEN	250o	150o	½ TO 1
SLOW OVEN	275o	160o	1 TO 2
VERY MODERATE OVEN	325o	170o	1 TO 2
MODERATE OVEN	350o	180o	3 TO 4
MODERATELY HOT OVEN	375o	190o	4 TO 5
HOT OVEN	400o	200o	5 TO 6
VERY HOT OVEN	450o	230o	8

C. ANGLO-INDIAN RECIPE BOOKS BY BRIDGET WHITE
(Presently in Print)

1. ANGLO-INDIAN CUISINE – A LEGACY OF FLAVOURS FROM THE PAST is a comprehensive and unique collection of recipes of well loved Anglo-Indian dishes such as Yellow Coconut Rice and Mince Ball (Kofta) Curry / Bad Word Curry, Pepper Water, Mulligatawny Soup, Pepper Steaks, Beef Country Captain, Ding Ding, Stews, Duck Buffat, Almorth, Brinjal Pickle etc, will take one on an exotic nostalgic journey to Culinary Paradise.

2. ANGLO-INDIAN DELICACIES (REVISED EDITION)
ANGLO-INDIAN DELICACIES is an interesting assortment of easy-to- follow Recipes of popular vintage and contemporary Cuisine of Colonial Anglo India. It covers a wide spectrum, ranging from typical English Roasts and Pasties to mouth watering Gravies and Curries, Pulaos, Savouries, Sweets, treats, etc. picking up plenty of hybrids along the way.

3. VEGETARIAN DELICACIES is a collection of simple and easy recipes of delectable Vegetarian Dishes. The repertoire is rich and vast, ranging from simple Soups and Salads, to mouth watering Curries, Stir fries, Rice dishes, Casseroles, Baked Dishes and popular Accompaniments. The book also highlights the health benefits and the goodness of each vegetable.

4. SIMPLE EGG DELICACIES is a collection of simple and easy recipes of delectable Egg Dishes for Breakfast, Lunch and Dinner and for all other times as well. The repertoire ranges from simple Breakfast Egg Dishes and Egg Salads, to mouth watering Curries, Tea Time treats, Sandwiches, Casseroles and Baked Dishes. The recipes are extremely easy to follow and only easily available ingredients have been suggested. - A real treat for 'Eggetarians'

ALSO BY BRIDGET WHITE: A nostalgic Book on Kolar Gold Fields entitled **KOLAR GOLD FIELDS DOWN MEMORY LANE – PAEANS TO LOST GLORY**! - A remarkable story going down memory lane for 125 years from the inception of the Gold Mines by the British Mining Company of John Taylor and Sons in the late 1800s till the 1970s.

D. ABOUT THE AUTHOR - BRIDGET WHITE-KUMAR

Bridget White-Kumar was born and brought up in Kolar Gold Fields, a small mining town in the erstwhile Mysore State (now known as Karnataka), in India, which was famous for its Colonial ambiance. She comes from a well-known Anglo-Indian family who lived and worked in KGF for many generations.

Bridget is a Cookery Book Author, Food Consultant and Culinary Historian. She has authored 7 Recipe books on Anglo-Indian Cuisine. Her area of expertise is in Colonial Anglo-Indian Food and she has gone through a lot of effort in reviving the old forgotten dishes of the Colonial British Raj Era. Her 7 Recipe books are a means of preserving for posterity, the very authentic tastes and flavours of Colonial 'Anglo- Indian Food' besides recording for future generations, the unique heritage of the pioneers of Anglo-Indian Cuisine.

Her Recipe Book ANGLO-INDIAN CUISINE – A LEGACY OF FLAVOURS FROM THE PAST was selected as 'Winner from India' under the Category: 'BEST CULINARY HISTORY BOOK'. by GOURMAND INTERNATIONAL SPAIN, WORLD COOK BOOK AWARDS 2012

Bridget is also an Independent Freelance Consultant on Food Related matters. She has assisted many Restaurants, Hotels and Clubs in Bangalore and elsewhere in India with her knowledge of Colonial Anglo-Indian Food besides helping them to revamp and reinvent their Menus by introducing new dishes which are a combination of both Continental and Anglo-Indian. Many of them are now following the Recipes and guidance given by her and the dishes are enjoyed by both Indian and Foreign Guests.

Bridget also conducts Cooking Demonstrations and Workshops at various places across the country such as Clubs, Restaurants, Women's Groups, Corporate Offices, etc. She is always ready to share and talk about Recipes and Food.

She can be contacted on +919845571254

Email: bridgetkumar@yahoo.com

http://anglo-indianfood.blogspot.com

http://anglo-indianrecipes.blogspot.com

http://bridgetwhite-angloindianrecipes.blogspot.com